UDL

MOVING *from* EXPLORATION *to* INTEGRATION

Edited by **Elizabeth Berquist**

CAST Professional Publishing

UNTIL LEARNING HAS NO LIMITS™

Library of Congress Control Number: 2017944244

Paperback ISBN 978-1-930583-00-9
Ebook ISBN 978-1-930583-01-6

Published by:
CAST Professional Publishing
an imprint of CAST, Inc.
Wakefield, Massachusetts, USA

For information about special discounts for bulk purchases, please email publishing@cast.org or telephone 781-245-2212 or visit *www.castpublishing.org*

Cover and interior design by Happenstance Type-O-Rama
Cover photo by Rawpixel.com/Shutterstock
Author photo by Kanji Takeno

Printed in the United States of America.

To Dr. David H. Rose,
for being the teacher so many of us need
and for inspiring us to be the same to others

Contents

SECTION 3: UDL IMPLEMENTATION IN SCHOOL SYSTEMS

Foreword

A re there any stories more exciting than those of pioneers? Pioneers are curious and daring. They are willing to cut new trails, travel unknown roads, sail uncharted seas. They inspire us, encouraging us to venture into places of discovery, wonder, and promise. They also inform, providing maps and reconnaissance, warnings and advice.

In this timely new collection, *UDL: Moving from Exploration to Integration*, Elizabeth Berquist has brought together some early pioneers of Universal Design for Learning (UDL) implementation. Although UDL was first defined in the 1990s at CAST—a nonprofit organization with a mission to make education more inclusive—the framework was largely applied to product design in those early years. Only in the past dozen years have serious efforts been made to infuse UDL into education practice in classrooms, schools, and school systems.

In this book, these pioneers discuss many important topics related to implementation, such as the need to build effective professional learning communities, to cultivate support among school faculty and parents, and to integrate UDL with existing initiatives so that it does not become just one more "flavor of the month." The authors—all proven leaders at the school, district, and state levels—don't mind forging into details to carve out paths of success for you, the reader.

Especially helpful is the discussion throughout of the need for a change in beliefs and mindset. UDL is a conceptual shift; rather than asking students to adapt to an inflexible curriculum via accommodations and retrofitted solutions, UDL expects that the curriculum will made flexible enough so it can adapt to the needs of variable learners (Meyer, Rose, & Gordon, 2014). To make such a shift in thinking is a tall order for educators. Prior beliefs and experiences—of educators but also of students and their parents—are not easy to change. Several chapters in this book provide helpful and realistic advice for how to foster and nurture such change in professional communities and in the community at large. The authors wisely understand that any sustainable effort to improve schools will require the buy-in and cooperation of all relevant stakeholders.

Who better to bring these authors together in one volume than Liz Berquist? Dr. Berquist herself was one of those pioneers, serving as one of Baltimore County's UDL facilitators when it participated in a national project funded by the Bill & Melinda Gates Foundation to explore UDL implementation. Dr Berquist is a talented educator who has been engaged in schools as a teacher, administrator, central office curriculum expert, and college professor. I have observed her excellence in all of these varied roles. She has the rare combination of academic and intellectual talent, engaging people skills, and total dedication to student and teacher success.

In 2012, while I was Maryland's State Superintendent of Education, Maryland became the first state in the nation to formally incorporate Universal Design for Learning into its education policies. In particular, the regulations called for integrating UDL principles into the development and provision of instructional methods and materials, assessment, and teacher professional development. Since that time, UDL has become increasingly become part of the larger conversation on education improvement. The Every Student Succeeds Act of 2015 and the National Education Technology Plan of 2016 endorse UDL implementation, and states and districts across the United States and Canada are putting the principles into practice.

As more and more educators take up the challenge to implement UDL, there will be new lessons learned and added to the literature. But this enterprising book is an excellent place to start that journey, filled as it is with wise and hard-won lessons from these UDL pioneers.

—NANCY S. GRASMICK, PHD

Preface

If I have seen further than others, it is by standing on the shoulders of giants.

— ISAAC NEWTON

I wonder if, when David Rose, Grace Meo, Anne Meyer, Skip Stahl, and Linda Mensing met in a Massachusetts pizza parlor in 1984 and set in motion the idea that became CAST (learn more at *www.cast.org*), they imagined that, thirty years later, an entire book would be dedicated to the implementation of the framework they developed or that their framework would be embedded in national policy that guides the practice of educators across the United States. In the past thirty-plus years since the Universal Design for Learning (UDL) framework made its entrance into the education field, CAST has worked diligently to blend high-quality research with thoughtful, proactive design to support the development of products and learning environments that improve education for all learners.

Maybe you are a reader just beginning to explore UDL because you have read one of the many texts describing the UDL framework and its applications, or maybe your interest was piqued by attending a workshop or training on UDL and you see it as a way to meet the challenges of learner variability. Maybe you are a classroom teacher who wants to implement UDL in order to reach more students in the margins, and you want to engage your colleagues in the process. Or, maybe you are a building administrator who sees value in using the framework to increase student engagement. You also could be a district- or state-level administrator wondering how to integrate UDL as a large-scale initiative. Regardless of your role, I believe you will find strategies and resources in this text that will help you build your plan to implement UDL.

This book attempts to answer the question "What does UDL implementation look like and how do we get there?" This question is most often asked following an introductory UDL training, and it is nearly impossible to provide a quality response in less than five minutes. Why is it so hard to answer? Because the implementation of UDL is variable and unique—in this sense, it is a model of UDL itself. UDL looks different in every learning environment, just as it looks different in every school, district, and state. Although there are patterns to be found in this variability, there is no one right way to implement the UDL framework. It is up to you, the reader, to learn from the experiences of others and build your own path.

CURRENT CONTEXT FOR UDL IMPLEMENTATION

Some chapter authors have decided to provide background on UDL, whereas others assumed that readers interested in a text on UDL implementation have a foundational knowledge of the framework. In the spirit of UDL, I feel it is necessary to activate the background knowledge of those readers who may need some additional context for UDL implementation.

CAST describes UDL as a framework to improve and optimize teaching and learning for all people, based on scientific insights into how humans learn. The UDL framework has evolved considerably since its inception more than thirty years ago, based on research in numerous fields, including developmental psychology, neuroscience, computer science, and architecture (Rappolt-Schlichtmann, Daley, & Rose, 2012). The framework of UDL has been further extended in books written by scholars at CAST: *Teaching Every Student in the Digital Age: Universal Design for Learning* (Rose & Meyer, 2002), *The Universally Designed Classroom* (Rose, Meyer, & Hitchcock, 2005), *A Practical Reader in Universal Design for Learning* (Rose & Meyer, 2006), and *Universal*

Design for Learning: Theory and Practice (Meyer, Rose, & Gordon, 2014). CAST created the UDL guidelines to support application of the UDL framework in the field, based on research from several disciplines.

The UDL framework recently was endorsed in the Every Student Succeeds Act of 2015 (ESSA), the current reauthorization of the Elementary and Secondary Education Act of 1965, which was originally developed to address the need for greater equity and opportunity in public schools. ESSA cites the definition of UDL first described in the Higher Education Opportunity Act of 2008:

> The term UNIVERSAL DESIGN FOR LEARNING defines a scientifically valid framework for guiding educational practice that
>
> > provides flexibility in the ways information is presented, in the ways students respond or demonstrate knowledge and skills, and in the ways students are engaged; and
> >
> > reduces barriers in instruction, provides appropriate accommodations, supports, and challenges, and maintains high achievement expectations for all students, including students with disabilities and students who are limited English proficient.

UDL is also highlighted in the 2016 National Educational Technology Plan published by the U.S. Department of Education, which sets out a vision and plan for learning enabled by technology and is aligned with the activities supported by ESSA. UDL is presented as a way to design and implement accessible curriculum and assessments for all learners in the "Learning" and "Assessment" sections of the plan. The Bartholomew Consolidated School Corporation (see chapter 8) is applauded as a district that has successfully embedded the UDL framework in its decision-making process in order to support all learners most effectively.

Learner variability is the norm in today's classrooms, and both ESSA and the *National Education Technology Plan* encourage educators to carefully consider how they will develop the content knowledge, skills, and attitudes that will enable all learners to reach their maximum potential. Each reference to UDL in current policy demonstrates that multiple means of engagement, representation, action, and expression will be woven into the fabric of future education and curriculum design. As the application of UDL continues to grow rapidly, we must determine how best to introduce the UDL framework into the professional development experiences of educators who are seeking to apply the framework to their practice. The chapters in this book present what leaders in the UDL field have experienced through the phases of implementation: exploration, preparation, integration, scaling, and optimizing. The book offers effective strategies for designing high-quality professional learning experiences to those responsible for introducing the UDL framework into their workplace or for moving from UDL awareness to integration.

OVERVIEW OF THIS BOOK

This book is divided into three sections that focus on (1) professional learning using the UDL framework, (2) UDL implementation at the school level, and (3) UDL implementation in the district and state. You may choose to read this book from start to finish or to consider each chapter individually. Although the chapters are designed to provide an overview of implementation from the micro to the macro level, there is no need to read them in order.

In "Section 1: Professional Learning the UDL Way," the authors describe how they successfully used the UDL framework in their practice as a lens to develop professional learning opportunities. In chapter 1, I explain how using a conceptual change-based instructional model can help those responsible for professional development to design more targeted instruction about the UDL framework. I also offer specific strategies for applying the UDL Guidelines to the design of professional learning and highlight the design process of some of the most talented presenters in the field: Loui Lord Nelson, Jon Mundorf, Katie Novak, and Kavita Rao. In chapter 2, Lisa Carey, Patti Ralabate, Bill Sadera, and I extend the discussion of using UDL to design professional learning by providing insight into coaching strategies that support professional learning communities. We summarize a study that explored change in teacher beliefs, knowledge, and practices, and describe how understanding participants' conceptions can have a positive impact on the design of professional learning. Chapter 3 offers a vision for designing online professional learning opportunities using the UDL framework. Lisa Katz, an outstanding instructional designer, explains the importance of designing with a digital learning mindset and makes a case for using UDL to develop high-quality online learning experiences.

In "Section 2: UDL Implementation in Schools," we turn to the application of professional learning in schools that are seeking to implement the UDL framework. Chapter 4, by Jennifer Mullenax and Nicole Fiorito, is a case study of how one elementary school built a culture of professional learning using the principles of UDL. This chapter clearly outlines a plan for guiding a staff to see the connection between UDL, professional growth, and student achievement. In chapter 5, Nicole Norris, who was principal at Lansdowne Middle during the Gates/CAST UDL implementation project and is the current principal at Prettyboy Elementary, shares Lansdowne's journey from UDL awareness to implementation. She describes how a UDL culture developed with the start of a small professional learning community and grew to become the driving force behind instructional improvements that impacted the entire school. In chapter 6, Rene Sanchez, Kirsten Omelan, and I describe a multiyear UDL project from the perspective of a collaborative leadership team consisting of regional staff, high school faculty, and UDL consultants. We demonstrate how a committed group of leaders and teachers can move UDL from being yet another initiative to become the central framework guiding a high school campus. Chapter 7 illustrates how co-teaching teams of general and special education teachers can use UDL for their inclusive classrooms. Kavita Rao and I demonstrate how co-teachers can apply UDL to goals, assessments, methods, and materials, and provide an example of a "co-teaching conversation" that illustrates how a general education and a special education teacher can incorporate UDL for a standards-based lesson.

"Section 3: UDL Implementation in School Systems" examines implementation at the district, state, and regional level. Chapter 8 is a collaborative effort by one of the most focused and goal-driven UDL teams in the nation: Rhonda Laswell, George Van Horn, Tina Greene, Angie Wieneke, and Jessica Vogel of the Bartholomew Consolidated School Corporation in

Columbus, Indiana. They share their process for district-level UDL implementation and, after eight years of implementation at Bartholomew, offer strategies on how to scale and optimize the framework. William Burke offers a large-district perspective on UDL implementation in chapter 9. He explains how implementing UDL across an entire district requires a strategic plan that aligns the work of many offices and departments. Burke describes strategies for embedding the UDL framework into the curriculum, material selection, and professional learning to build a learner-centered environment. Finally, in chapter 10, UDL leaders in Maryland describe how the state became the first in the nation to adopt legislation focused on UDL. They explain how a state department can support UDL implementation, and then highlight these efforts in selected districts.

Are these the only examples of UDL implementation in practice? Of course not! Such efforts are taking place across the United States and around the globe. The examples highlighted in this book are just that—examples designed to give readers ideas about how to move from the initial exploration of UDL to full-scale implementation. There is no right or wrong way to begin implementing UDL, but the experiences and examples shared in this text, when taken as a body of work, can provide a strong foundation to guide your own journey. The UDL framework encourages us to communicate, collaborate, and build community. Those of us active in the UDL field are adamant about sharing and supporting one another, so as you review these chapters, take away the points that will help you to grow and do not hesitate to build on the foundation laid by others to help you go further—we certainly have.

Section 1

Professional Learning the UDL Way

1

Using the UDL Framework as a Guide for Professional Learning

Elizabeth Berquist

GUIDING QUESTIONS

- How does the Universal Design for Learning (UDL) framework guide professional learning?

- Why is it important to understand educators' current conceptions of UDL when designing professional learning experiences?

The purpose of this chapter is to share the experiences of educators who have utilized the Universal Design for Learning framework to design professional learning opportunities that have moved schools, districts, and states from an exploration of UDL to integration and, ultimately, scaling. Like students, educators vary in the ways they engage with content, in how they perceive information, and in the strategies they use to make sense of what they know. Professional learning opportunities must recognize and address this variability. This chapter provides a rationale for using a conceptual change model to explore educator conceptions about teaching and learning, and identifies specific strategies for designing short (one- or two-day) professional learning experiences that are aligned with the UDL framework.

INTRODUCTION

Consider this scenario. Your district or school has decided to introduce the UDL framework as a way to meet the needs of diverse learners, for the following reasons: the framework is found in numerous federal policies and documents designed to guide decision making (Every Student Succeeds Act, 2015; Higher Education Opportunity Act, 2008; U.S. Department of Education, Office of Educational Technology, 2010, 2016); school districts are sharing data that support increased student achievement since they adopted UDL (Nelson, Arthur, Jensen, & Van Horn, 2011); and some states have adopted UDL in their curriculum development process (e.g., Code of Maryland Regulations [COMAR], 2012). After your district or school has decided to implement UDL, a group of administrators and practitioners attend a mandatory professional development session to learn about UDL. The UDL framework is presented, the background described, the Guidelines distributed, and the educators are then sent back to their classrooms to apply their new knowledge. Will these educators begin to espouse the benefits of UDL and apply the Guidelines in their classrooms?

The literature tells us that the answer is no. For real change to occur, learners must progress through a series of stages, during which they come to alter their beliefs (e.g., Dole & Sinatra, 1998; Pintrich, Marx, & Boyle, 1993; Posner, Strike, Hewson, & Gertzog, 1982; Tillema & Knol, 1997). In the previous scenario, no attempt was made to identify educators' underlying assumptions, beliefs, or knowledge about the use of UDL, and the design and delivery of the professional development session made no attempt to model the UDL framework.

We must confront the challenge of developing effective professional learning experiences by moving the conceptual change process and the proactive application of the UDL framework to the forefront of the instructional design process. The first step in successful UDL implementation is to design high-quality professional learning experiences that consider the power of educators' existing conceptions, and to model the UDL framework in action. In this chapter, we discuss the importance of addressing educator beliefs in a professional learning setting and provide strategies for designing professional learning experiences that align with the UDL framework.

Loui Lord Nelson, UDL consultant and author of
Design and Deliver: Planning and Teaching Using the UDL Framework

UDL is always in the forefront of my mind as I'm designing any professional development (PD). When I fully understand the outcomes the partner organization is seeking, I'm able to nail down the goal for the PD. From there, I begin working through the knowledge and skills (essentially, standards) I want the participants to have when they leave. At this point, I've already been thinking about activities, strategies, and formative assessment pieces that I'll use throughout the PD, but I continue to circle back to be sure that they (a) align with the goal, and (b) are designed using the UDL Guidelines to ensure they are accessible to all learners. Most importantly, there is no perfect UDL PD or lesson. This leaves room for the development of new ideas and improved accessibility. At the end of each PD, I return to my plan, reflect on the outcomes my learners achieved, and seek ways to improve upon the design.

WHAT IS UNIVERSALLY DESIGNED PROFESSIONAL LEARNING?

The golden rule when presenting on UDL is to model it in your practice. No participant wants to attend a workshop where the facilitator talks about engaging learners with multiple options for representation or for action, and then uses a 500-slide Microsoft PowerPoint presentation to share their message. If you want your participants to develop a deep understanding of UDL, they must experience the framework as a learner. It is also helpful to be explicit about the design of your workshop. Don't be afraid to step out of presentation mode to display the design of the UDL framework and to point out where you have applied specific UDL Guidelines in your training session.

Learning Environment

One of the biggest misconceptions about UDL is that it is all about a lesson or unit plan. Yes, UDL does impact lessons and units, but it is more powerful to apply UDL first to the overall learning environment. The Partnership for 21st Century Learning (2009) describes the learning environment as a support system that organizes the conditions under which humans learn best. They encourage educators to design environments that accommodate the unique learning needs of every student by carefully considering structures, tools, and communities. This is a departure from the traditional conception of a learning environment as a static space, and it sounds a lot like the UDL framework.

Applying the UDL framework to your learning environment calls for careful, proactive planning that requires you to consider access to learning, scaffolds, and opportunities for students to become expert learners. Identifying options that occur regularly in your learning environment will automatically enhance your lesson plans because you will have identified many of the barriers to learning that educators face daily and set out to remove those barriers.

In the context of a professional learning session, designing the learning environment starts with the presentation space. The room should be set up for collaborative work. Chairs in rows, for example, are not conducive to discussion, so participants should sit at tables or place the chairs in a U shape so they can see one another. It is critical to create a space that all participants can navigate comfortably, such as posting direction signs within the building or ensuring that there is enough space to move easily between chairs and tables. It is also essential to know participants' names to make them feel welcome, which can be done by providing nametags or creating table tents with cardstock and markers. Music and visual enhancements can make the space inviting; for example, you can use chart paper to post agendas or motivational quotes, or to give participants a place to post questions—the beauty of the UDL framework is that there is no one "right way" to design the space.

Jon Mundorf, P. K. Yonge Developmental Research School at the University of Florida and National Board Certified Teacher

UDL provides a framework to design for the systematic learner variability present in all learning environments. Designing with the UDL principles gives learners multiple means of engagement, representation, action, and expression to become expert learners. Traditional professional learning design tends to focus on the mythical average learner and prevents most learners from optimal learning. Instead of a traditional design approach that combines a one-size-fits-all learning goal and activity, UDL begins with a clear goal and allows for flexible means so that each learner finds appropriate challenges and supports. The flexibility can occur within goal, the methods, the materials, and/or the assessments. When I design for the variability present in a group, I begin by reflecting on the purpose of the professional learning experience I'm planning. Once I determine the purpose or goal, I then consider the different pathways participants could travel to accomplish the goal. I also try to anticipate potential barriers that may prevent participants from making progress. Formative assessments along the way help me to monitor progress and, when appropriate, summative assessments provide information to allow me to reflect on instruction and learning.

Goals

Creating the learning environment is followed by curriculum planning, which must consider the "big four" of the UDL framework: goals, assessments, materials, and methods. Like UDL, the professional learning session should focus on goals, which can be determined by asking, "What is your overarching goal for the workshop? How will you articulate this goal to the participants? How will participants develop goals for their own future learning?" It is also wise to set smaller objectives for each section of the professional learning session. For example, if the overarching goal is to "apply the UDL framework and principles to learning environment design," the day should be broken up into smaller sessions that focus on such objectives as "explain the structure of the UDL framework, principles, and Guidelines" and "explore examples of UDL practice in authentic learning environments." All goals and objectives should be clearly articulated in a written agenda that is available to all participants.

It is also important to provide multiple pathways to achieve these goals. Meyer, Rose, and Gordon (2014) remind us that "traditional curriculum planning focuses heavily on content or performance goals," whereas the aim of UDL curriculum planning is to develop expert learners. In planning the professional learning experience, consider how to enable your participants to identify the resources and supports they will need to continue learning on their own.

Assessments

Once you have identified the overarching goals and objectives for your professional learning session, you should outline your assessment plan. The UDL framework favors formative assessments that are part of the instruction (Meyer, Rose, & Gordon, 2014) and provide a way to determine learners' progress toward the goals; this is as important in professional learning as it is in the classroom. If we complete an entire workshop without knowing if participants are making sense of new information, we run the risk of furthering misconceptions or leaving educators frustrated. It is important to tell participants how and why you are measuring their understanding of the content and let them know you will use that information to guide your instruction. This is also an opportunity to model flexible assessment methods, which can get participants moving and enable you to gauge their understanding. There are countless ways to embed formative assessments in your professional learning toolkit, and many free Web 2.0 assessment tools are available online.

Katie Novak, K–12 administrator and author of numerous books about Universal Design for Learning

When designing PD [professional development], it's critical to empower educators to contribute to the design…so they can experience the power of collaboration, feedback, and learner voice. Before designing options in my school district, I make sure to listen to educators so I know exactly what they need in order to personalize their professional development. I share this information by using multiple means of representation, and I encourage multiple means of expression in their responses. I'll send [them] an email with a video link where they can hear me explain the importance of their feedback, or they can just read an email. Once they understand why their feedback is critical, they can share their thoughts through a Google Form, they can email or call me, or they can tell me face-to-face when I drop into each school for my annual "PD Road Show." As a next step, I foster collaboration and community by thematically coding teacher needs with a PD committee, which consists of…elementary and secondary [teachers] in multiple content areas. We ensure that, as we design our PD calendar, every educator has options to allow them to meet their goals. In our district, we offer graduate courses,…opportunities for independent study, course reimbursement, book groups, and professional learning communities. All teachers literally design their own PD calendar. After each session, teachers reflect and provide mastery-oriented feedback about how we can improve. As a PD committee, we use that information to design new strategies for future PD. It's a cycle that is learner-centered, flexible, and constantly improving.

A summative assessment measures a learner's performance once instruction is complete, usually to hold educators accountable (Meyer, Rose, & Gordon, 2014). Most of us equate a summative assessment with end-of-unit tests or high-stakes standardized assessments, the intent being to evaluate the effectiveness of your instruction relative to a set of standards. In a professional learning setting, summative assessments may be used to measure the goals outlined on the original agenda. I recommend creating a formal evaluation that asks participants to provide a quantitative rating and qualitative feedback for each of your goals and objectives. Once you analyze this data, you can determine what types of professional learning the group may benefit from in the future. You can also use this information to determine if your instruction was effective. We are all aware that a typical summative assessment—multiple choice, fill-in-the-blank, or short-answer tests—often creates barriers in the classroom because they offer learners few options for expression. I am always seeking to create summative assessments that are aligned with the UDL framework, as even the smallest changes can make a difference for our learners. Consider offering the assessment tool both on paper and online.

Materials

Selecting flexible materials for your professional learning session is another way to apply theory to practice. When considering materials, think about using tools and media both to present content and to provide ways for participants to interact with new material and demonstrate what they have learned. Although the UDL framework can certainly be applied in low-tech or no-tech environments, we have learned that digital media enable us to put many of the UDL Guidelines into practice. Using an online platform to organize your session resources may offer your participants greater options for perception than printed materials because they can customize the display of information or use features such as text-to-speech and synchronized highlighting to make the information more readable. Organizing materials in a logical sequence online provides scaffolding and support and helps to manage resources. Many online sites offer opportunities for social interaction, which promotes community and collaboration. The way you organize your materials should mirror the kind of support participants would expect in face-to-face and online environments. Finally, as all good teachers know, a backup plan is always necessary. Be sure that you have hard copies of presentation materials in case the Internet is not functioning, and for participants who are not comfortable navigating online.

Individuals responsible for professional development should also consider how participants will interact with the workshop materials. Prior to your session, think about what you want participants to know and how they will demonstrate that knowledge. Gather a variety of materials for action and expression and be sure to offer both low-tech (sticky notes, chart paper, markers, and index cards) and high-tech options (there are several free online tools). Many materials will meet this need; the key is to identify those your participants can also use with their students.

Methods

Meyer, Rose, and Gordon (2014) explain that "...because learners vary in the ways that they become and stay motivated to learn, comprehend information and strategically approach tasks, the UDL framework emphasizes the need to employ many kinds of teaching methods" (p. 77). An effective professional learning session should include the same instructional strategies used in a high-quality lesson plan—goals, assessments, flexible materials, and flexible instructional methods—and should offer an engaging opening and a focused closing that summarizes the lesson. The most important element is a well-defined instructional sequence. Regardless of the instructional format, it is essential to provide access, scaffolding, and options for students to become expert learners. The UDL framework provides a lens for assessing the elements provided in your session.

UDL AS A CONCEPTUAL CHANGE

UDL is a framework that forces educators to reconsider what they know about curriculum and instruction. However, a few best practices are available for designing instruction about UDL, a lack that is problematic, since systemic UDL implementation is already in progress at schools and universities across the nation (Rappolt-Schlichtmann, Daley, & Rose, 2012). A major challenge of existing professional development and university coursework is the lack of attention they give to the existing beliefs administrators, teachers, and preservice teachers.

In recent years, research in the learning sciences has evolved, new and flexible resources have been designed, and the UDL framework has changed from a theoretical tool to an actionable construct (Rappolt-Schlichtmann, Daley, & Rose, 2012). Arguably, one of the most critical shifts in the development of the UDL framework was the conclusion that students were no longer the problem, and that the existing educational environments were too narrow to meet the diverse needs of learners in today's classrooms (Rose & Meyer, 2002). Much of UDL's foundation, such as building options into the curriculum from the start or teaching students to be expert learners rather than expert students, may contradict traditional educators' beliefs about teaching and learning. I have personally observed, for example, that individuals' experiences and beliefs can exert a powerful influence on what and how they learn. I believe that instruction based on conceptual change can help those responsible for professional development to understand the power of people's existing beliefs about UDL, and thus enable them to design more targeted instruction about the framework.

All learners enter formal educational settings with strong ideas based on prior experiences (Dole & Sinatra, 1998), and a conceptual change model can help them alter their beliefs (Posner et al., 1982). Learners' existing beliefs can create barriers when they are exposed to a new concept, like UDL, which may be inconsistent with their long-held ideas. They cannot modify or advance these beliefs unless they progress through the stages of conceptual change. The original model of conceptual change proposed by Posner et al. (1982) was designed to help learners alter their beliefs by progressing through four specific stages: dissatisfaction, intelligibility, plausibility, and fruitfulness.

Educators who are dissatisfied with their current approach to solving a problem often seek professional development about UDL. They may be looking for ways to close achievement gaps or meet the needs of students in the margins. Those who initiate professional learning about UDL may already be in the dissatisfaction stage, but this does not mean that the rest of their professional learning group will be on board. We all have been to professional learning sessions where some participants are unsure why they are attending or how a new framework will fit into their work. Using conceptual change-based instructional strategies can be instrumental in helping skeptical educators understand the UDL framework and embrace it as a way to design flexible learning environments that support all learners.

Kavita Rao, Associate Professor, University of Hawaii

I begin the design process by considering how to make the best use of the time I have in a class or training session. I "chunk" the time I have down into smaller spans (twenty–thirty minutes) and design activities for each span. Within each span, I consider how I will use the UDL Guidelines to make sure I present information in various ways, highlight key points, give participants a chance to develop and apply what they are learning, and express their own understanding of the concepts being taught. Within each span, I provide varied options and scaffolds so that participants have many choices and modalities as part of their learning experience. Most importantly, as I design each workshop, I try to put myself in the shoes of the participants, imagining the varied preferences, interests, and needs of people, and ensuring that I plan activities that are likely to draw everyone in (if not at the same time, at least over the course of the training).

Educators' experiences in conceptual change-based learning environments can help them understand their existing beliefs and become motivated to accept UDL as a plausible, fruitful framework for meeting the challenge of learner variability. Numerous strategies exist for employing the conceptual change model in teacher education. Tillema and Knol (1997) developed an instructional sequence for preservice teachers that I have found useful in designing professional development about UDL.

This process consists of activating prior knowledge, introducing new information, promoting the active exploration of new learning approaches, strengthening understanding, and exchanging ideas. I have modified this process for a one- or two-day "introduction to UDL" workshop, but conceptual change in fact takes time and is best suited to an extended professional learning experience.

Activation of Prior Experiences

When introducing any new framework, it is critical to first take time to identify learners' existing conceptions. This is especially relevant when introducing UDL, as many of the foundational assumptions differ from what is considered traditional instruction (Rappolt-Schlichtmann, Daley, & Rose, 2012). We often hear, for example, that UDL is "one more thing," the "same as differentiation," or that it requires "access to technology at all times" and is "only a support for students with disabilities." When participants have misconceptions about the UDL framework and have not had the opportunity to address them, they cannot move forward in understanding and applying the framework. It is important to note that, when encouraging participants to share their viewpoints, you are fostering a sense of community and collaboration in your session, which is one of the checkpoints in the UDL Guidelines.

Introducing New Information

Once participants have been exposed to the idea that variability is the norm, they often wonder how they can meet the challenge of that variability and if they will be expected to plan differently for each learner in their classroom. Maybe the group has been designing with a reactive approach—essentially, planning for the middle and coming up with alternatives when students do not succeed. To help participants reframe this practice, you can ask them to share a problem that relates to meeting the needs of diverse learners, and use the ensuing discussion as a springboard for introducing the UDL framework as tool for meeting the needs of all learners. Using a video or a text that defines learner variability and presents UDL as a way to meet this challenge has been very effective. In his TEDx talk on variability, Harvard neuropsychologist Todd Rose explains:

> From the perspective of UDL, we can identify three dimensions of systematic variability that will exist in every learning environment at every age. And those are differences in terms of the way that people represent information, differences in the way that they engage with material, and differences in the way they can act upon material and show what they know.

Participants in your professional learning session should discuss how to identify patterns of variability; this will establish an excellent foundation for introducing the UDL Guidelines as a vehicle for identifying patterns in learners.

Promoting Active Exploration

According to the National UDL Center, the UDL Guidelines should help educators plan learning environments, goals, methods, materials, and assessments that "reduce barriers, optimize levels of challenge and meet the needs of all learners from the start." Just as we encourage teachers to provide their students with options, those providing professional learning sessions should offer participants ways to explore and implement the Guidelines. There are a variety of ways to do so, from the original text-based versions, to the UDL Wheel created by Maryland educators, to the UDLinks app available through iTunes. As Bill McGrath, a UDL leader from Montgomery County, Maryland, reminds us, "UDL is a lens, not a list." It is imperative that you make this clear when introducing the UDL Guidelines, principles, and checkpoints to participants.

Educators should be given time to explore the UDL Guidelines. It can be beneficial to break the participants into groups and work together to express each guideline in "classroom" language. When first introduced to the Guidelines, participants often identify barriers to their implementation, such as time constraints, challenges with the existing curriculum, or a lack of resources. It may be helpful to provide examples of the UDL Guidelines being applied in authentic learning environments. Remember that you may be presenting a very different picture of a classroom than your participants are accustomed to, and the challenge will be to provide opportunities to compare their beliefs, knowledge, and practices with what they are learning about UDL. This is also an opportunity for you to model how to run small-group or station instruction. If you organize your materials online before the session, the structure will enable participants to work independently online while others work with the facilitator.

Strengthening Understanding

By this point in the professional learning session, participants should begin to see UDL as a reasonable framework for designing learning environments and curriculum. A frequent criticism of professional learning is that educators are not given time to process new information and are forced to integrate new knowledge into their practice without time to explore and prepare. Therefore, when designing your instruction, include time for learners to build a personal understanding and knowledge base about UDL (Sadera & Hargrave, 2005), as this will help them adopt changes. Also consider ways to make the new practice relevant to your participants. For example, encourage classroom teachers to use the nine Guidelines to self-assess their current practices that align with the UDL framework. Have them identify areas for growth and use the National UDL Center resources to address areas of need. Participants also can identify technology tools that support the integration of the UDL principles or practice writing lessons using the Guidelines. Curriculum developers may want to review their materials to identify possible barriers, and then develop a structure for using the Guidelines to remove such barriers in advance of instruction. Administrators could design in-service sessions where they model the Guidelines for their faculty, and collaborate with teacher leaders to develop formative classroom "look-fors" (or characteristics that leadership expected to see in classrooms) based on the UDL framework. Regardless of what position your participants hold, it is essential to engage them in learning activities that relate to their work.

Discussion and Exchange of Ideas

At this stage of the professional learning session, participants' knowledge base should be expanded by self-reflection, discussion, and sharing ideas.

This process can help you evaluate whether participants' understanding of UDL has changed and, if so, why. Learning activities at this point may include engaging in small-group discussions after watching video of teachers in classrooms where multiple options are the norm: these examples provide a stark contrast to the traditional intervention model, which should prompt rich discussion of the UDL framework's power to meet the needs of all learners. Such experiences will help participants begin to see the UDL framework as intelligible, plausible, and fruitful. Finally, participants should always be asked to assess the workshop, which not only shows that you value their feedback but enables you, the facilitator, to make changes in your instruction or delivery, if needed.

CONCLUSION

The professional learning options described in this chapter are a starting point for further exploration of conceptual change and universally designed professional development. To facilitate educators' growth in understanding and applying UDL, school and district leaders and individuals responsible for systemic professional development must work to create powerful and dynamic instruction that will prepare educators to implement the UDL framework in their classrooms and schools. Designing and integrating this type of instruction is a challenging and critical task, also one that is both timely and necessary, given current efforts to embed UDL in classrooms across the United States (Rappolt-Schlichtmann, Daley, & Rose, 2012).

Fixsen, Naoom, Blase, Friedman, and Wallace (2005) contend that the development and identification of evidence-based school improvement practices has made great strides but that the process for sustaining these initiatives is lacking. One reason for this lack of sustainability may be that educators are asked to make changes in their schools or classrooms without first confronting their existing beliefs about practice. Another barrier occurs when educators are told about best instructional practices but never have the opportunity to experience those practices as learners. Clearly, assessing educators' knowledge, beliefs, and practices is an essential component of any UDL implementation process (CAST, 2012). However, we too often present educators with new information without giving them an opportunity to consider how this knowledge relates to their current conceptions. Identifying, recognizing, and articulating educators' existing beliefs and modeling the UDL practices that we expect them to embrace are essential steps in planning high-quality professional learning experiences that support UDL implementation.

2

Changing Beliefs: A View Inside a Coaching Experience Based on UDL

Elizabeth Berquist, Lisa Carey,
Patti Kelly Ralabate, and William A. Sadera

GUIDING QUESTIONS

- What is a Universal Design for Learning (UDL) professional learning community (PLC)?

- How do UDL coaches address the three UDL principles?

- UDL requires teachers to adopt new concepts. How does that encourage PLC members to articulate their beliefs about teaching and learning, and to transform these ideas into practice?

The purpose of this chapter is to illustrate the effectiveness of applying UDL to coaching strategies for a professional learning community. We specifically explore the change in teachers' beliefs about their teaching skills and their students' learning abilities.

FIRST STEP: BUILDING A PROFESSIONAL LEARNING COMMUNITY

A fifteen-year veteran middle school teacher, Lauren always receives excellent evaluations. However, her district recently adopted a new teacher evaluation tool that includes her students' test results. Typically, Lauren's class is quite diverse: 47 percent of her students receive free and reduced-price lunches, nearly 13 percent receive special education services, and approximately 4 percent are English language learners. Although most of her students meet proficiency levels on the annual assessments, there are always some who don't. Lauren realizes that the performance of those few students who aren't learning well or aren't able to show what they know on a standardized test can now impact her evaluation. A reflective teacher, she is interested in finding ways to hone her instructional practices to reach more students effectively. She hears about a new district coaching initiative using a UDL approach and decides to find out more about it.

Lauren doesn't realize that she is about to embark on a coaching journey, one that will enhance her teaching practice through peer-to-peer learning. She also doesn't anticipate the impact UDL will have on her students. During the next year, a lot will change, including her beliefs about her role as an educator. Her first step is to volunteer for the new professional learning community (PLC) created by her principal to focus on UDL implementation. She is joined by twenty-two other middle school teachers, whose years of experience range from five to twenty-five years. Twenty of these teachers are certified in various content areas, including math, science, social studies, English, and physical education; two are special educators; and at least half have earned a master's degree in education. Lauren's principal, who is optimistic about the UDL coaching initiative, explains that, although the district has been exploring UDL for over a decade, it has not yet carried out a true implementation. In partnership with CAST, the nonprofit research and development organization that originated the UDL framework, the district has designed a new professional learning system that is based on using coaching practices that align with the UDL framework. The district offers incentives to encourage participation in this professional learning experience, including stipends for time spent and course credit for academic work completed during the project.

Each UDL PLC consists of cross-discipline teams whose emphasis is on reading and writing across content areas. The teams agree to meet weekly to learn how to infuse the UDL framework into their classroom instruction using a lesson-planning approach. Each team member completes a survey that includes questions about the UDL framework, how UDL is applied to classroom practice, and the teachers' beliefs about learning and student potential. The UDL PLC is guided by Emily, a UDL expert who serves as a coach and facilitator. She introduces them to the elements of the UDL framework and offers examples of UDL classroom practice.

Emily explains that UDL is a framework for teaching and learning that offers all individuals equal opportunities to learn (Hall, Meyer, & Rose, 2012). The Every Student Succeeds Act of 2015 (ESSA), the seventh reauthorization of the Elementary and Secondary Education Act, includes both a definition and an endorsement of UDL. ESSA uses the definition of UDL first described in the Higher Education Opportunity Act of 2008: a "scientifically valid framework for guiding educational practice" that is derived from research on neurodiversity and the learning sciences, and that provides educators with a structure for developing goals, materials, methods, and assessments that meet the needs of a wide range of learners by including flexible instructional options at the outset of the instructional design process (Higher Education Opportunity Act, 2008). UDL is recognized as being appropriate for all learners and is highlighted in the introduction to the Common Core State Standards, the National Education Technology Plan (U.S. Department of Education, Office of Educational Technology 2010, 2016), and the National Instructional Materials Accessibility Standard (CAST, 2011).

According to Rose and Meyer (2002), UDL is based on three broad principles, which are aligned with three brain networks that are involved in the learning process: (a) multiple means for presenting information to students (corresponding to the recognition networks); (b) multiple means for student action and expression (corresponding to the strategic networks); and (c) multiple means for student engagement (corresponding to the affective networks).

Using the UDL principles, educators have choices about how they present information, how their students may respond or demonstrate their knowledge and skills, and how their students engage in learning. A series of guidelines and checkpoints associated with each principle help educators design instruction that meets students' needs, and take into consideration the natural variability that exists in all classrooms (CAST, 2011). Figure 2.1 provides an illustration of the UDL framework.

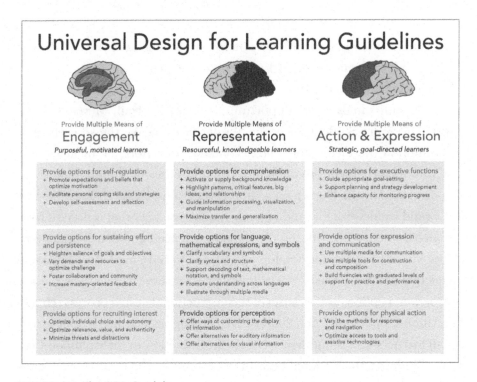

FIGURE 2.1 The UDL Guidelines   © CAST, 2014. USED WITH PERMISSION

Assessing UDL Knowledge, Practice, and Beliefs

To gain an understanding of teachers' preconceptions, practices, and beliefs about the teaching, learning, and implementation of UDL, all the educators involved in the Baltimore County UDL PLCs are asked to complete the CAST UDL Knowledge, Practice, and Beliefs (KPB) survey, which consists of seventeen items in three sections: Beliefs, Beliefs and Practice, and Knowledge and Practice. Teachers rate their level of agreement with statements such as, "I believe that all students can learn in general education settings," and "I believe that there is a range of learning variability in students in any educational setting." The Belief and Practice and Knowledge and Practice sections are similar in design, in that each uses a Likert-type scale:

> In my teaching practices, I: DO NOT plan to do this; am WILLING TO LEARN more about this so I could do this; PLAN to do this; do this OCCASIONALLY; do this SOME OF THE TIME; do this MOST of the time.

Teachers also are asked to provide written examples of their current practice (see Figure 2.2 for one example). The instrument is designed to gather data on what teachers know about UDL and then measure what parts of it they plan to apply or are currently applying in their practice. By having participants provide options on their own, rather than choosing from a list, the data provide a more accurate assessment of the teachers' beliefs and practices. The PLC coaches then use the survey results to design coaching sessions and to measure changes in educators' practice.

---

11. I believe all students can benefit from having multiple curricular options or learning pathways.

Level of Agreement

	Am not sure at this time	Strongly Disagree	Somewhat Disagree	Somewhat Agree	Agree	Strongly Agree
As an educator, I	○	○	○	○	○	○

Level of Practice

	I DO NOT plan to do this.	I am WILLING to LEARN more about this so I could do this.	I PLAN to do this.	I do this OCCASIONALLY (≤33%)	I do this SOME of the time (34-66%)	I do this MOST of the time (67-100%)
In my teaching practices	○	○	○	○	○	○

I provide multiple curriculum options for the benefit of all students using the following practices:

FIGURE 2.2 A question from the CAST UDL Knowledge, Practice, and Beliefs survey © CAST, 2012. USED WITH PERMISSION.

The UDL KPB survey data indicate where teachers' beliefs lie along the conceptual change continuum and, more specifically, where they are regarding the stages of dissatisfaction. UDL coaches use this information to develop strategies that accommodate new ways of thinking about students and instruction. For example, Emily notes that Lauren indicated some dissatisfaction with her current instructional practice—namely, that many students seem disengaged from the material and she is concerned that she is not reaching all her students. Based on this point, Emily is able to design instructional sessions that will enable Lauren and her fellow UDL PLC members to explore how UDL can help Lauren design lessons that meet the needs of all her students. Emily uses guiding questions to help Lauren sort out her shifting beliefs about instructional design and move toward a more nuanced understanding of the UDL framework. UDL coaches use the UDL KPB survey at the end of the year to identify what changes have occurred among UDL PLC members.

A Shift from Traditional Professional Learning

Lauren finds the UDL PLC experience different from the professional development workshops she has experienced before. Traditional professional learning usually consists of what Wei and colleagues (Wei, Darling-Hammond, Andree, Richardson, & Orphanos, 2009) call the "traditional one-shot model of professional development" (p. 58). In the traditional model, teachers attend individual workshops scattered throughout the year to learn about specific instructional techniques, subject-area approaches, or grade-level curriculum strategies. There is little to no follow-up. Unfortunately, the one-size-fits-all professional development that is conducted in isolation from daily practice forces teachers into passive roles, and it offers no time for reflection and collaboration is still the norm for many school districts (Varela, 2012).

Lauren's district in Baltimore County, Maryland, like numerous school systems throughout the United States, has focused its professional learning on UDL as a framework for meeting the challenges of learner variability and for designing high-quality curriculum (Hall et al., 2012). The real key to changing practice is high-quality, ongoing professional learning provided through PLCs, which offers an environment that is contextually supportive and collaborative. PLC meetings are designed to mirror UDL instructional practices. Rather than providing a large amount of direct instruction, Emily, the UDL coach, facilitates Lauren's PLC exploration and asks guiding questions. Lauren and her PLC colleagues are asked to revamp their expectations of what students should know and be able to do. While developing this vision, Lauren and the others are also asked to teach in new ways.

At first Lauren is surprised. Reconsidering beliefs and practices—in essence, learning to unlearn long-held skills and perspectives—is a challenging task not currently included in most professional development. According to Darling-Hammond and McLaughlin (2011), a significant component of teacher professional development is "accomplishing the serious and difficult tasks of *learning* the skills and perspectives assumed by new visions of practice and *unlearning* the practices and beliefs about students and instruction that have dominated their professional lives to date" (p. 81). To engage teachers in the complex process of changing their conceptions, professional development should focus on changing their beliefs, knowledge, and practices. It is impossible to accomplish this without first considering the conceptions about UDL that educators bring to the professional development experience (Berquist & Sadera, 2015).

CONCEPTUAL CHANGE: A SHIFT IN FOCUS

Applying the survey results along with the conceptual change framework gives coaches insights that help them design and develop instruction about UDL and identify appropriate strategies to move educators from exploring the framework to integrating it into their practices. Learning that changes an existing conception—a belief, an idea, or a way of thinking—is generally referred to as conceptual change (Posner, Strike, Hewson, & Gertzog, 1982). Conceptual change differs from other types of learning because it is not measured by the acquisition of a specific skill set or the ability to demonstrate factual knowledge, but by a shift in one's ideas and beliefs. It is a method for accommodating new knowledge and belief structures (Tillema, 1997); understanding and successfully applying UDL, for example, requires a conceptual change (CAST, 2010).

Educators traditionally have focused on designing instruction that meets the needs of "average" students, whereas UDL recognizes that there is no average, that "average" is an illusory concept. While Lauren's classes have always consisted of diverse learners, instructional expectations focused on teaching the average student. She therefore designed lessons she believed would work for most of her students. Students with disabilities, English language learners, and gifted and talented students were considered separately from the rest of the class, and some of her lessons included retrofitted accommodations in an attempt to meet their needs. Expectations have shifted with her district's new teacher evaluation system, and Lauren is now held responsible for making sure all her students grow academically. Lauren's PLC coach helps her see the problematic logic behind designing instruction to meet so-called average learners. As they review student data, Lauren realizes that none of the "average" students fit neatly into one profile. In recognizing the variability among her students, Lauren can see why it is important to determine if the curriculum and materials are causing barriers for some students, rather than viewing those students as problematic learners. Lauren is now able to design or redesign instruction that meet the needs of diverse learners, thereby shifting her focus from trying to alter students to changing the curriculum (CAST, 2010).

Sadera and Hargrave (2005) argue that changing existing beliefs occurs in the following stages: pre-dissatisfaction, dissatisfaction, and post-dissatisfaction. During the dissatisfaction stage, it is essential that PLC members compare new concepts to their existing beliefs. Understanding PLC members' degree of dissatisfaction with their existing beliefs allows UDL coaches to design targeted professional learning. For example, if PLC members are found to be in the pre-dissatisfaction stage, coaches should focus on addressing their beliefs about ability and disability. The team members could be challenged to acquire knowledge about the UDL principles and the corresponding brain networks in order to compare such new information with their current conceptions. If PLC members are in the dissatisfaction stage and have begun to realize that their current conceptions are not adequate to address the challenges presented by learner variability, professional learning should focus on leveraging the UDL framework to create flexible goals, materials, methods, and assessments.

Lauren immediately recognizes that the UDL PLC is a departure from traditional models of professional learning because it requires teachers to confront their current beliefs, construct their own knowledge, and participate in inquiry-based collaborative experiences that support corresponding shifts in thinking. The new information Lauren receives about variability within the student population makes it clear that all students do not learn in the same way or at the same pace. Faced with challenges to her current instructional practice, Lauren is forced to reassess her beliefs, and she thus begins the process of conceptual change.

UDL Coaching Leads to a Change in Beliefs

Four themes emerge from analyzing the UDL KPB results: (1) challenges in the written curriculum; (2) teachers' competency in identifying options; (3) barriers to the assessment process; and (4) teachers' willingness to learn more about UDL. On the conceptual change continuum, all these results are indicative of the dissatisfaction stage, which is characterized by questioning the validity of current beliefs (Sadera & Hargrave, 2005). UDL coaching is designed to address the three UDL principles by offering (a) multiple ways for teachers to build their knowledge, (b) multiple choices that engage and sustain the participants' interest over time, and (c) multiple instructional strategies for each instructional barrier that is revealed, which teachers can immediately apply to their planning. Embedding the UDL principles in coaching sessions helps Lauren and her PLC team members confront their existing conceptions. Over time, Lauren becomes keenly aware of her beliefs about instruction and realizes that her current solutions to the challenge of learner variability are not adequate, which is an essential part of the process of moving toward a new practice. Acknowledging this evolution of beliefs among UDL PLC members has significant implications for coaches attempting to change teacher practice.

Coaching sessions are designed to help PLC members articulate their beliefs about teaching, learning, and UDL, and to transform these ideas into practice. For example, Lauren has learned to identify common practices in the district's curriculum that are barriers to learning, such as using the same text for the entire class. Although she believes this one-size-fits-all text cannot meet the diverse needs of her students, she previously had been unsure of how to deal with the challenge. The UDL coaching sessions heightened her awareness of alternatives. For example, instead of beginning with the same text for all students and providing alternatives only to those who are unsuccessful, her PLC coach suggested that Lauren offer multiple texts from the beginning as a more effective way to address learner variability. Deliberate learning activities, such as explicit instruction on how to tier readings and scaffold initial assignments, help Lauren and other PLC members move past the dissatisfaction stage. See the accompanying sidebar, "Professional Learning Experiences Designed to Encourage Use of the UDL Framework," for additional examples of professional learning experiences designed to shift teacher beliefs, knowledge, and practices to align more closely with the UDL framework.

Professional Learning Experiences Designed to Encourage Use of the UDL Framework

The following examples of professional learning experiences are designed to shift teacher beliefs, knowledge, and practices to align with the UDL framework. It is essential that UDL coaches model the UDL principles by offering multiple means of engagement, representation, action, and expression across all PLC sessions.

Representation

- Teachers benefit from experiencing the UDL principles as learners. By offering multiple means of representation for UDL PLC materials and engaging in group discussion about personal preferences and needs, teachers witness the value of flexibility and choice.

- Create an online site to host all materials. UDL Connect is an excellent tool for sharing and organizing agendas and resources (see *http://community.udlcenter.org/*).

- Post instructional materials and resources in addition to providing hard copies.

- Offer PLC members a choice of online or digital UDL text (e.g., *Universal Design for Learning: Theory to Practice* at *http://udltheorypractice.cast.org/login*).

- Offer a variety of resources for individual and group exploration in multiple media formats.

- To support understanding within a specific context, model UDL-style exercises in teachers' classrooms.

Engagement

- Continually seek feedback from PLC members in order to make ongoing adjustments to professional learning.

- Provide time for colleagues and other educators to see UDL in practice by coordinating classroom-classroom, school-school, and district-district observations.

- Link UDL PLC work to teacher-evaluation systems and the expectations of the school administration (see examples in the Charlotte Danielson UDL Crosswalk, posted on the National UDL Center website at *www.udlcenter.org*).

- Ask teachers to identify barriers to UDL implementation and address these barriers in PLC meetings, as well as in the form of individualized in-time supports as necessary.

- Support teachers' executive function by asking guiding questions.

- Co-teach with novice UDL practitioners to offer support and modeling.

- Ask PLC members to discuss their expectations of UDL implementation with their appraisers, and collaborate to determine PLC and school goals.

Action and Expression

- Help the UDL PLC set group goals for their joint learning and instructional practices.
- Guide teachers in setting and tracking individual goals for their professional development, and provide in-time support to help attain these goals.
- Provide options for PLC member collaboration, such as UDL Connect, on-site PLC meetings, and virtual phone or multimedia sessions.
- Make it possible for PLC members to engage in professional learning opportunities in conjunction with PLC meetings (e.g., to attend conferences, or participate in UDL Twitter chats).
- Enable PLC members to demonstrate changes to their professional practice.

Lauren's UDL coach has determined that her PLC group's beliefs are not always consistent with their practices. Although they offer definitive positions on topics such as providing students with multiple curricular options or learning pathways, the results of the UDL KPB survey indicate that these teachers do not necessarily provide these options in their practice. For instance, Lauren is aware of the inconsistencies in her beliefs and knowledge and recognizes that her conceptions differ from her practice. She believes that offering students a choice in how they demonstrate mastery increases their engagement, but she isn't sure how to assess differing lesson products. To help her with this challenge, the UDL coach explores how to design rubrics that maintain high expectations by measuring the same content standard, while also giving students choices in how they demonstrate their knowledge and mastery of the standard. By applying the UDL framework, the coach gives Lauren and her team members opportunities to compare, contrast, and evaluate their beliefs, knowledge, and practices.

From Novice to UDL Coach

By the end of her UDL coaching experience, Lauren realizes that her beliefs and instructional practice have undergone a significant change and that her beliefs now align with her practice. She is able to plan instruction that meets her students' needs, and she knows how to measure their progress. In fact, Lauren now feels confident enough to take on the role of UDL coach. She is excited to share what she has learned and is eager to help other teachers move beyond the dissatisfaction stage. She starts by having them confront their existing beliefs and uses the UDL framework to support their process of change. As she guides her UDL PLC, Lauren's coaching is grounded in understanding teacher beliefs, knowledge, and practices. In stark contrast to traditional professional development, her coaching offers professional learning that includes flexible options, concrete examples, and the opportunity to learn from peers who are on the same journey.

3

Designing Digital Learning: Bringing UDL to Life Online

Lisa Katz

GUIDING QUESTIONS:

- How do we leverage web-based tools and online learning platforms to reduce barriers and provide access to learning for all students?

- How do we leverage the power of digital media to support students in becoming expert learners?

This chapter describes the importance of developing a digital learning mindset and discusses strategies for selecting flexible materials for digital learning. It also introduces Universal Design for Learning (UDL) as a framework to support learning with technology.

DESIGNING DIGITAL LEARNING EXPERIENCES WITH UDL IN MIND: THE BASICS

Bringing technology-rich resources to instruction makes sense in a society that increasingly depends on technology to communicate, share ideas, and collaborate. However, we in the field of education have a way of jumping headfirst into new initiatives without first considering the implications for students or their learning. Technology can seem like a quick fix for classroom challenges, as though the newest device or interactive whiteboard will work magic.

Learning should be dynamic and engaging, and technology can often be applied to help accomplish this. The growth of online social networks for educators and their students; the creation of digital narratives via Snapchat, Instagram, and other social media; and the growth of augmented reality (tagging static objects and content with interactive materials to bring content to life) can enhance the learning experience and create deeper meaning for students and adult audiences.

But digital learning should be built on solid instructional design and practice, which involves making personal connections, collaborating with other students and teachers, and providing interactive instruction. Universal Design for Learning (UDL) can help us accomplish this by providing framework for making effective digital learning experiences.

UDL is a framework for improving and optimizing teaching and learning based on scientific insights and research of how humans learn (Rappolt-Schlichtmann, Daley, & Rose, 2012). The framework helps educators design flexible and adaptive learning environments, which can lead to deeper student learning and higher achievement. According to the National Center on Universal Design for Learning website (2012), UDL implementation is "not a set of discrete steps or protocols that everybody does in exactly the same way. It's a process: an iterative, continuously improving cycle of learning, reflection, and growth. In this way, you can customize the supports that are provided to districts in order to meet their unique needs."

UDL is built around three core principles: providing multiple means of engagement, representation, and action and expression. These principles are grounded in brain research, technological advancements, and classroom experiences. When educators are aware of and able to use the UDL principles to address systematic learner variability, students will become more engaged in the content and begin to make connections between emotion and cognition. Table 3.1 describes how these principles are connected to learning in the brain and the delivery of instruction.

TABLE 3.1 Brain networks and application to instruction

BRAIN NETWORKS	DESCRIPTION OF THE NETWORK	UDL PRINCIPLE	APPLICATION TO INSTRUCTION
Affective	The affective network supports learning engagement and motivation; it evaluates patterns and assigns them emotional significance; and it enables humans to engage with tasks and learning and with the world around us.	Multiple Means of Engagement	Instruction should tap into student strengths, interests, and motivations to support meaningful and applicable learning.
Recognition	The recognition network supports learning acquisition and comprehension; it enables humans to identify and interpret patterns of sound, light, taste, smell, and touch, and to assign meaning to the patterns we see; and it enables us to gather facts, categorize what we see, hear, and read in learning.	Multiple Means of Representation	Instruction should provide presentations that share information and content in different ways to support resourceful and knowledgeable learning.
Strategic	The strategic network supports learning acquisition and comprehension; it enables humans to identify and interpret patterns of sound, light, taste, smell, and touch, and to assign meaning to the patterns we see; and it enables us to gather facts, categorize what we see, hear, and read in learning.	Multiple Means of Action and Expression	Instruction should allow for differentiated assessment and knowledge-sharing to support strategic, goal-directed learning.

Source: Meyer, Rose, & Gordon, 2014.

Embracing UDL requires a shift in mindset, as other articles in this book have demonstrated. Moving to a digital curriculum from using primarily print-based resources also requires a mindset shift (Ray, Laufenberg, & Bejerede, 2016). In *A Guide to Choosing Digital Content and Curriculum*, published by the Center for Digital Education, Ray, Laufenberg, and Bejerede call this change in mindset "profound":

> Technology offers students the opportunity to take ownership of their learning, and enables teachers to accommodate a more student-centric learning environment. Digital content, tools and curriculum support this shift by allowing students to collaborate, work at their own pace, access various resources and extend their learning beyond the four walls of the classroom. (p. 7)

Many factors come into play when preparing for and implementing a digital learning mindset, but what is it? Educators who have adopted a digital mindset describe it as follows:

- The teacher is not the sole source of information in the classroom.

- One-size-fits-all learning is the way of the past. Personalizing learning is important to support student engagement and deep learning.

- Flexibility and adaptability are key to learning.

- Collaboration between and among students is central to learning.

- Students are the creators and producers of digital content.

- Access to learning materials and resources is open and available.

- Digital content is relevant to students' lives.

- Taking risks when learning is encouraged.

Once the new mindset is embraced and ideation, prototyping, and experimentation become the norm, the selection and implementation of digital materials can begin in the classroom. Having a new mindset, however, is not enough. Careful instructional design and modification of the learning environment also should be part of preparing for digital learning in the classroom (see sidebar).

Guiding Principles for Digital Design

Some years ago, the Maryland State Department of Education, Howard County Public Schools, and Prince George's County Public Schools worked with the design consultancy IDEO to learn more about how technology can support student learning, course design, and teacher professional development. This research identified seven guiding principles to help educators design for today's learning environment and align their instruction to UDL. The following table shows these principles and UDL connections. To learn more about this research project, view these videos about the Design Thinking Process (*https://vimeo.com/35570482*) or 21st Century Learning Report Findings (*https://vimeo.com/35572900*).

CONNECTIONS BETWEEN GUIDING PRINCIPLES AND UDL

GUIDING PRINCIPLE	UDL CONNECTION
Empower students to have a voice	Multiple Means of Engagement; Action/Expression
Connect to real life	Multiple Means of Engagement; Representation
Focus on the process, not the outcome	Multiple Means of Engagement
Build in time to reflect and grow	Multiple Means of Engagement
Leverage technology in meaningful ways	Multiple Means of Representation; Action/Expression
Engage learners on multiple levels	Multiple Means of Engagement; Representation
Support teachers to try new things	Multiple Means of Engagement; Representation; Action/Expression

DESIGNING INSTRUCTION FOR DIGITAL LEARNING

Have you ever planned a meal with new ingredients that you really thought were going to complement each other, and then it just didn't turn out? The marriage of sound instructional design and digital content is like that elusive perfect meal—you can plan for it, but the recipe can only get you so far. Based on the guests' tastes and allergies (variability) and the cooking conditions (instructional design), modifying the recipe as you cook usually gets you a better result. This section will investigate the "recipe" for instructional design, blended learning, and the strategies and digital tools that support the principles of UDL.

Knowledge of the components of instructional design should provide the foundation on which everything is built. So, what is instructional design and how does it relate to the UDL principles and framework? Instructional design is defined as "the practice of creating instructional experiences which make the acquisition of knowledge and skill more efficient, effective, and appealing" (Merrill, Drake, Lacy, & Pratt, 1996, p. 2). Instructional designers identify the needs of the learner and the goals of instruction, and then apply instructional supports to help learners acquire the desired knowledge and apply what they learn. Robert Gagné was an American educational psychologist who trained pilots for the Army Air Corps during World War II. He is best known for his 1965 book, *The Conditions of Learning*, in which he established instructional design principles, and for developing the Nine Events of Instruction (Gagné, Briggs, & Wager, 1992) and applying them to computer and multimedia learning. The nine events include:

- Gain attention

- Provide a learning objective

- Stimulate recall of prior experience

- Present the material

- Provide guidance for learning

- Elicit performance

- Provide feedback

- Assess performance

- Enhance retention and transfer

Gagné's model of instructional design is based on the "mental events that occur when adults are presented with various stimuli" (Khadjooi, Rostami, & Ishaq, 2011). Gagné's Nine Events of Instruction are set up to support creating a structure for learning using the goals and measureable outcomes. As Gagné himself said, "Organization is the hallmark of effective instructional materials" (Khadjooi, Rostami, & Ishaq, 2011, p. 116). As a theory of instructional design, Gagné's work has helped inform other methodologies that instructional designers use to create training materials, online courses, and digital content. The Nine Events of Instruction can be aligned with the UDL principles and each of the brain networks as they relate to the implementation of the instructional strategies and in the design and planning for instruction. For example, in planning for ways to gain and hold students' attention, educators are tapping into the affective network. When stimulating the recall of prior knowledge, presenting information, and providing guidance, educators are providing multiple means of representation. When students are asked to show what they know, self-reflect, relearn, or apply learning to new situations and offer feedback on the lesson, multiple means of action and expression are at work.

SELECTING MATERIALS

When an educator, school, or district has adopted a digital mindset, the next step is to determine which materials will best support the instructional practices they plan for their students. Digital content should engage students, provide multiple means of representation, and allow for flexible assessments so students can show what they know.

The Center for Digital Education provides a list of the types of digital content that should be reviewed and implemented in a classroom with digital learners (Table 3.2), which includes UDL as a guiding framework for digital learning. UDL supports planning for digital learning in the classroom and help teachers "take advantage of the opportunities inherent in the great variability of students, offering paths for those currently disenfranchised and developing the talents of all" (Meyer, Rose, & Gordon, 2014, p. 84).

TABLE 3.2 Recognizing good digital content

CONTENT ELEMENTS—HOW IS CONTENT REPRESENTED?	
Graphics	Does the content include visuals, images, and graphics that complement and support the text?
Interactive elements	Do students interact with the content by selecting text or scrolling through multiselect options? Is the interactive content engaging?
Flexible assessments	Do the assessments feature a variety of options and styles to vary the way outcomes are measured? Are students given the opportunity to review and evaluate their work and progress?
FUNCTIONALITY—HOW DOES THE DIGITAL RESOURCE/CONTENT WORK?	
User interface (UI)	Is the user interface fluid, easy to navigate, and intuitive for all users?
Data collection	Does the digital content collect data via assessments, or are they built into the system so that the learner's understanding is captured?
Interoperability	Do data flow seamlessly between learning applications?
Adaptive engines	Do the learning management tools utilize the data collected through student and teacher interaction to create and/or support personalized learning paths?
LEARNING MODALITIES—HOW DOES A STUDENT ENGAGE WITH THE CONTENT?	
Learning paths	Do the students have multiple pathways to learn the information? Can they choose how they learn the material? Are the pathways based on levels of mastery measured through formative assessments?
Cognitive load	How much are you asking students to do? (More work does not equal rigor. Too much stimulation and too many activities can overwhelm for the learner.)
Self-paced	Is learning self-paced, and can students work through the material while mastering content at their own pace?

Adapted from Ray, Laufenberg, and Bejerede (2016, p. 9)

BLENDED LEARNING AND FLIPPED CLASSROOMS: A CASE STORY

Blended learning refers to "any formal education program in which a student learns at least in part through online learning, with some element of student control over time, place, path and/or pace" (Horn, Staker, & Christensen, 2015, p. 43). Most blended learning opportunities involve an integrated learning experience, where face-to-face learning and the acquisition of online content work together to enhance student comprehension and understanding.

Many models exist for blended learning, but the most popular is the *flipped classroom.* In a flipped classroom, students review and learn content independently (Multiple Means of Representation: perception), and when students are with the teacher, instruction is built on their self-regulated content acquisition. Thus, instead of using class time for direct instruction, the teacher can use it to provide instructional support and workshops to go deeper on some of the concepts, or to conduct applied labs and projects. Providing an option for students to view, pause, and rewind content videos based on their skill development and mastery puts their learning in their own hands and gives them more ownership over learning the content. Said one middle school math teacher who took part in a flipped classroom study in Idaho, "In some ways, it feels less...teacher-ish. You have to redefine how you see yourself as a teacher" (Horn, Staker, & Christensen, 2015, p. 44). The mindset shift accompanied a change in practice.

How can UDL be applied in the flipped classroom? Let's consider the following case story to explore that question. Anthony DeStefano is a middle school science teacher. He is learning about UDL and is excited to apply what he has learned about the brain networks to teaching and learning in his classroom. He begins by activating students' prior knowledge and tapping into their recognition networks. To do this, he gives students a Kahoot (*www.kahoot.it*)—an online formative assessment tool—to stimulate students' recall about the forms of energy and to identify patterns in those forms.

After this preassessment, he opens a bag of freshly popped popcorn and tells students they will be watching a video of a concert while they enjoy the popcorn.

He asks them to note different things they sense—the heat of the popcorn, the sound of drums—while experiencing the popcorn and music video, and to post them on a Padlet (*www.padlet.com*), an online cork board for sharing ideas.

Later, the students work in small groups to choose one of their observations and create a mini-poster, a song, a report, or another type of display to present the object; identify what type of energy was being produced; and explain where that energy came from. For example, they show that the heat from the popcorn came from the microwave, which got its energy from electricity, which came from a power plant, and so on.

Students are then instructed to watch a YouTube video Mr. DeStefano created explaining key vocabulary and other information about energy transfer. Students watch the video at home and take notes on key concepts, and then meet in small groups in class to compare and evaluate their notes. (To see some of the videos go to *https://goo.gl/SwIdGg*. Subscribe to Mr. DeStefano's channel to learn more about science. He used *http://ezvid.com* to develop and record the videos.)

For the last related assignment, students complete an online activity to track the flow of kinetic and potential energy from one object to another. This activity shows each form of energy and allows students to complete the pathway step by step. Students then post a screenshot of their work to a group Google Doc so other students can see it.

How do Mr. DeStefano's learning experiences model good instructional design (ID) and incorporate UDL? While he embedded digital tools throughout his lesson, he also flipped the instruction to allow students to customize and pace their learning and collaborate with others outside of class time. Table 3.3 shows how his design aligned to the UDL principles.

TABLE 3.3 UDL case story: Tasks and applications of ID and UDL

STUDENT TASK	INSTRUCTIONAL DESIGN AND UDL APPLICATIONS
Preassessment/prior knowledge via *www.kahoot.it*	Gagné: Stimulating Recall of Prior Knowledge UDL: Multiple Means of Representation to promote resourceful and knowledgeable learners

STUDENT TASK	INSTRUCTIONAL DESIGN AND UDL APPLICATIONS
Stimulating the senses and engaging learners to introduce the concepts	Gagné: Gaining Attention UDL: Multiple Means of Engagement to promote purposeful and motivated learners
Sharing ideas on *www.padlet.com* about the popcorn activity and energy	Gagné: Eliciting Performance UDL: Multiple Means of Action and Expression to promote strategic and self-directed learners
Watching the video about energy transfer developed by the teacher for direct instruction	Gagné: Presenting Information UDL: Multiple Means of Representation to promote resourceful and knowledgeable learners
Group work to debrief the video	Gagné: Providing Guidance UDL: Multiple Means of Action and Expression to promote strategic and self-directed learners
Complete the online activity about energy and post screenshots to the Google Doc	Gagné: Assessing Performance UDL: Multiple Means of Action and Expression to promote strategic and self-directed learners

Just as there is no one way to present information and represent content, there is no one way to deliver instruction and professional learning via digital means. Tools can refer to both analog and digital, and good design likely combines the two to meet the needs of their learners in the classroom. Technology tools and resources are learning supports; they do not replace sound instructional design and practice. Modeling UDL through the selection of digital materials and designing lessons so they can be accessed in a variety of ways via options for perception and comprehension is critical. Use sample teacher or student products to showcase applications and model for students. The accompanying sidebar highlights some digital tools and resources that can assist with providing multiple means of representation and action and expression in the classroom.

Turning Eighth-Graders Inside Out

While participating in the worldwide Inside Out Project, a middle school art teacher named Mr. Katz created an interdisciplinary unit in collaboration with humanities teachers to bring his students' photo essays to life via augmented reality. Using the augmented-reality app Aurasma, Mr. Katz turned his students' photographs (see the following graphic) into interactive artistic statements. Here Mr. Katz explains the purpose of the assignment and how the use of technology created an opportunity to attach student reflections recorded on videos, attached to two-dimensional work, creating an interactive experience for the viewer.

> Being a middle school student, it is sometimes difficult to find your place in a community. At our school, we want to hear from our students, but also encourage them to act on their beliefs; to get involved. By asking student artists to share their thoughts, we hope to spark richer expression, a clearer opportunity to have one's voice heard, and an overall empowerment that might otherwise be denied or overlooked. Young people need to have an outlet. The Inside/Out Project can give them a platform and ask them to be brave.
>
> In this project, students wrote an artist's statement, videotaped themselves using an iPad, and connected the video they created to their photograph. When displayed, it looks like a large photo, but when you apply technology, the artwork comes to life, as the artist's statement is read by the student in the image. This is multiple means of representation and action and expression in action!

To view Mr. Katz's students' work, visit *www.insideoutproject.net/en/group-actions/usa-annapolis-maryland-2*. If you want to listen to the students' statements, follow the directions below to download Aurasma, follow the channel, and then watch the content come alive when you hover the app over the image.

GETTING STUDENTS INVOLVED AND ENGAGED

In this section, we will review the importance of student engagement, how to leverage web-based tools, and how to use dynamic content creation tools to reduce barriers and provide access to learning for all students. When referring to tools, they can be both digital (e.g., computers, tablets, adaptive software) or analog (e.g., sticky notes, manipulatives, colored blocks).

UDL is a key component in supporting digital learning solutions that center on flexibility, authenticity, and collaboration. Providing multiple means of engagement is a UDL principle that is central to the success of representation and action/expression. Providing options for perception, comprehension, and action/expression increases individual choice and autonomy, minimizes threats and distractions, and optimizes relevance, value, and authenticity by promoting executive functions and self-regulation. Engagement is critical to deep and meaningful learning (Meyer, Rose, & Gordon, 2014).

Students told the magazine *Edutopia* (Wolpert-Gawron, 2015) that engaging learning environments include the following:

Collaboration   Working with peers

Technology   Using digital resources

Real-World Connections   Project-based learning and making real-world connections to content

Relationships and Being Human   Teachers loving what they do and connecting with students

Interactivity   Get me out of my seat!

Make It Visual   Show graphics to support the text

Student Choice   Allow students to choose how they learn the content, assignments, and options for assessment

Understand Student Strengths   Encourage students to be themselves and bring their best selves to learning

Mix It Up   Provide multiple means for students to learn content

When students know and understand their strengths, they can find a way into the learning experience, remain persistent when facing a challenge or failure, and continue to build self-knowledge.

One great idea from the book *Amplify: Digital Teaching and Learning in the K-6 Classroom* (Muhtaris & Ziemke, 2015) is to create a digital recording booth to capture student learning and progress. In the classroom, the teacher uses a computer, tablet, or other device to record student learning, feedback, and/ or feelings about a lesson or topic. One example is a video book review for and by students that can be shared with others to support literacy and excitement about reading. By modifying the traditional formative assessment, the teacher is providing multiple means of action and expression—specifically providing options for expression and communication (UDL Guideline 5).

"By allowing kids to record video book reviews and making them accessible on a website or blog, we build community in which kids know they have an audience for their work" (Muhtaris & Ziemke, 2015, 17).

Teacher Spotlight: Engagement and Goal-Setting in the Classroom

Providing multiple means of engagement involves tapping into students' affective network and supporting their motivation and purpose for learning. Brittney Briggs is a fifth-grade teacher who writes a blog that has a lot of great ideas for the classroom—and she models UDL! One of my favorite activities is "Keep the Quote," which was proposed by a student. A goal-setting activity, students bring in quotes to propose as the classroom motto for the week. The students share their quotes, and the one selected is posted in the classroom. At the end of the week, the class reviews the success of the motto. One student gets to keep the posted motto as a way to recognize and celebrate the variability among students (Briggs, 2016). You can also follow Brittney on Instagram to see her other great ideas for the classroom: *https://www.instagram.com/miss5th/*.

COURTESY OF BRITTNEY BRIGGS. USED WITH PERMISSION.

Mrs. Hallowell, a second-grade teacher, attended a UDL training as a part of a professional development series. Learning about UDL seemed to be redundant, something Mrs. Hallowell already knew how to do. After all, as part of the preK–2 team at her school, strategies and supports for students are inherent in the way they teach content. Providing multiple means of representation and action and expression was something she knew she did well with traditional materials.

One activity she engaged in as part of her professional development was to examine a lesson or series of lessons to identify barriers to learning. She chose to tackle the engagement barrier and to offer her students multiple means of action and expression using digital tools she learned about in the trainings. She slowly introduced Google Docs and other collaborative online tools to her second-grade students to augment the learning she had already planned, and she saw their engagement soar. When she asked students to share what they liked, they said, "I liked this year's learning different ways to do math, so then I know different ways to check my answers and can solve other types of problems."

As the year went on, she went from whole-group augmentation with collaborative tools to personalized learning for all students, while modifying the learning goals to support content mastery with student choice. Some students chose to use Google Docs to share ideas, whereas others chose more traditional means, and still others explored topical online games for independent practice.

At the end of the year, she asked her students to reflect on their learning: "I asked reflection questions to kids at three different levels…and the surprising part for me was to see how much insight they had about themselves as learners and what worked for them and what didn't as part of our lessons. They could identify, in ways that my students have never done before, what they needed, and how the lessons helped them learn."

CONCLUSION

Classrooms, schools, and universities across the world are facing design challenges every day that hinder innovation: from evaluation systems, to learning spaces, to access to reliable and mobile learning, to affordable and modular higher education opportunities. In many classrooms and academic institutions, we are teaching students to follow recipes—take notes, regurgitate information, take point-in-time assessments—rather than to create, discover, and imagine new possibilities. "In the rapidly expanding capabilities of digital content, tools, and networks, we see the possibility of conceiving, designing and delivering a curriculum that will accommodate widely varying learner needs" (Meyer, Rose, & Gordon, 2014, p. 128). How can we have the deep change needed for a transformation in teaching and learning without innovative learning solutions? Learning should be dynamic and engaging, and include technology as it applies to the learning goals and design of instruction.

This chapter outlined the importance of a digital learning mindset, selecting appropriate materials for digital learning, and using technology to support UDL implementation. Digital learning can and should build using UDL as an overarching framework to support instructional design. This design for learning should take into consideration the type of digital content and how the resource or tool enhances learning, builds engagement through personal connections, ensures collaboration with other students, and provides dynamic and interactive content for all learners.

Bonus! Learning Solutions with Digital Tools

Here are some cool digital resources you can use today to improve teaching and learning in your universally designed classroom.

Multiple Means of Representation

Are you interested in changing how you present information? Interested in having students learn content independently? Check out the following digital resources that can help you represent content in new and different ways.

Animoto (*https://animoto.com/*)—Create thirty-second videos to introduce content or summarize learning. View a sample here: *https://vimeo.com/70910590.*

Wideo (*www.wideo.co/en/*)—Make animation videos for your presentations, teaching lessons, or just to have some fun.

TES Teach (*https://www.tes.com/lessons/gallery*)—TES Teach is a digital library of presentations, portfolios, and projects.

Google Arts & Culture (*https://www.google.com/culturalinstitute/beta/u/0/project/art-project*)—Take your class on a field trip to a museum in Paris. Master works of art are captured and can be viewed in the galleries and in close-ups.

ThingLink (*https://www.thinglink.com/*)—This interactive media platform allows static images to be animated with images, video, or text.

TedEd (*https://teded.herokuapp.com/*)—Build lessons, share content, and create assessments measuring understanding.

Instagrok (*www.instagrok.com/*)—Research any topic; create an interactive concept map and share.

Visuwords (*www.visuwords.com/*)—An online graphical dictionary.

Quozio (*http://quozio.com/*)—Turn quotes and words into beautiful images.

Symbaloo (*https://www.symbaloo.com/*)—Virtual bulletin board for apps and websites providing quick links to resources for students.

Word Clouds—Visual representation of text using keyword metadata

    Word It Out: *http://worditout.com*

    Tagxedo: *www.tagxedo.com*

    WordArt.com: *https://wordart.com/*

Google Cardboard (*https://www.google.com/get/cardboard/get-cardboard/*)—Cardboard is an analog device that attaches to a smartphone to allow virtual reality apps to be displayed. Virtual reality apps allow students to interact with content via virtual reality.

Here are a few apps to try with Cardboard:

Virtual Reality Stories from *The New York Times*: *https://goo.gl/VwCpWx*

Titans of Space: *https://goo.gl/iWtMqf*

Discovery VR: *https://goo.gl/MAvsTl*

Within-VR: *https://goo.gl/4urFTo*

DinoTrek VR Experience: *https://goo.gl/v23Fde*

Orbulus: *https://goo.gl/Yq2PU6*

Polar Sea: *https://goo.gl/ucEtOF*

Google Cardboard Camera: *https://goo.gl/FDcroh*

Google Expeditions—This virtual reality field trip tool works in conjunction with Google Cardboard. The app allows teachers to guide students through an exploration of 200 (and growing) historical sites and natural resources in an immersive, three-dimensional experience. Watch how one museum is using augmented reality (n.d.) to make the experience interactive at *https://www.youtube.com/watch?v=v_cvAGUItU0.*

Multiple Means of Action and Expression

The following digital resources can help you support student expression, self-assessment and reflection, and executive functioning.

Digital Storytelling

These tools provide options for expressive skills and fluency:

Google Story Builder (*https://docsstorybuilder.appspot.com/*)—Easily create video stories.

Storybird (*https://storybird.com/*)—Reverses visual storytelling by starting with the image and "unlocking" the story inside. Explore artists to select their work for your book, get inspired, and write. Check out this sample book: *https://storybird.com/chapters/the-mystery-of-dogwood-cross/1/.*

Screencastify (*https://www.screencastify.com/*)—If you are interested in recording a demo, webtouring websites, or narrating a presentation, try Screencastify, an extension for Google Chrome. You can also use it to capture videos that you cannot download or save. Recordings are limited to ten minutes and are saved to Google Drive.

AwwApp (*https://awwapp.com/draw.html*)—A touch-friendly whiteboard app that let's users use their computers, tablets, or smartphones to create, collaborate on, and share drawings.

ToonDoo (*www.toondoo.com*)—*Lets users make and share comic strips.*

Digital Assessment and Feedback

These tools provide options for executive function by providing guides and checklists and/or providing opportunities to share questions and feedback.

Kahoot (*www.Kahoot.it*)—An online assessment tool.

AnswerGarden (*https://answergarden.ch/*)—Online brainstorming and feedback tool.

Plickers (*https://plickers.com/*)—Real-time formative assessment tool.

Flippity (*http://flippity.net/*)—Allows teachers to easily make a Jeopardy-style game for students to review and practice.

Digital Cork Boards

These tools provide options for content acquisition and sharing and allow students to use sticky notes to share information on a virtual wall. These "cork boards" or "walls" can be made public or private, and can be used to support learning activities such as Socratic seminars, fishbowls, and video debriefs.

Lino.it—*http://en.linoit.com/*

ListThings—*http://listthings.com/canvas*

Padlet—*www.padlet.com*. Check out this sample Padlet from a UDL training about barriers to learning: *https://padlet.com/lisapkatz/aj7xirkk7usn.*

Section 2

UDL Implementation in Schools

4

Establishing a Culture That Values Twenty-First-Century Professional Learning

Jennifer Mullenax and Nicole Fiorito

GUIDING QUESTIONS

- What impact does the culture of a building have on student achievement?

- How can the Universal Design for Learning (UDL) framework help create a culture that values professional learning?

This chapter focuses on how to create a school culture that understands the correlation between UDL, professional growth, and student achievement. This begins by recognizing that all learners—students and teachers alike—exhibit the full range of human variability, and that one-size-fits-all approaches don't apply in the classroom or in professional learning. The Halstead Academy's professional learning offered a model of professional learning that provided a supportive, knowledge-rich community for practitioners.

RECRUITING CHANGE AGENTS

A new school year is always an exciting, energizing experience for students, parents, teachers, and administrators. For the new Halstead Academy principal, this year was not only exciting but eye-opening. This new principal had been assigned to an urban Title I school that was labeled the lowest achieving elementary school in a system of 110 schools. Thus she was eager to see what was happening that prevented students from being successful. As she walked through the building the first week of school, she could tell the school would benefit from developing a shared vision and building more collaborative relationships. The principal began holding meetings at which she helped staff members identify what roles they would play in moving the school forward. Although she was enthusiastic about engaging staff in these potential changes, several teachers were reluctant to see themselves as change agents.

This was particularly true with Mrs. B., an intermediate classroom teacher, who believed her teaching ability was among the best in the school. She was confident in her instruction and did not feel she would benefit from professional learning opportunities. Based on her informal and formal observations, the new principal decided to have a conversation with Mrs. B. and offer her a few options to help her refine her craft.

One dreary fall afternoon, the principal entered Mrs. B.'s empty classroom and asked to discuss some opportunities she thought would interest the teacher. Mrs. B. grudgingly agreed to talk. The principal offered several professional learning opportunities, such as peer observation, lesson studies, professional development sessions, and several books, but Mrs. B. refused them all. The principal couldn't understand why a teacher, a person who should value learning, would decline opportunities to grow and learn. How could she resist an opportunity to build her instructional toolkit?

Mrs. B. clearly was struggling to understand how this scenario could be beneficial and expressed concern that many of the opportunities offered would take her out of the classroom and cause students to miss instructional time. Even after the principal spent an hour explaining the positive impact effective professional development can have on student achievement, the two could merely agree to disagree. Unfortunately, the principal found that many of Mrs. B.'s concerns were common among the school's staff, but she had other ideas of how to help her teachers embrace this essential component of quality teaching.

The principal realized that she needed to help her staff understand and appreciate the correlation between their professional growth and student achievement. She also recognized that the teachers were at very different places in their learning and would benefit from setting goals related to their own growth, which would also benefit students. She decided that her first step would be to identify her own goals for the school, establish clear expectations, and hold individuals accountable for their role in the growth of the school. Her goals were simple: (a) make Halstead a learning community, (b) change the negative perception of the school, and (c) become a Blue Ribbon school, an honor given to schools that demonstrate academic excellence or close achievement gaps. She based these goals on the high expectations she set for herself, the staff, the students, and the school community. Although guided by these personal goals, the principal did not share them publicly, because she knew the staff would need to embrace them gradually. Over time her plan became more manageable because she continually aligned her decision-making process with the goals.

To operationalize these broad goals, the school staff needed to recognize what Novak (2014) identifies as the four ingredients students need to learn: the student's own effort, the social context in which the child exists, the opportunity to learn, and good teaching. The teachers needed to understand their role in offering students these four ingredients and, more importantly, to embrace the concept of learner variability. Variability is the norm in all classrooms, and teachers' plans to meet learners' varied needs must begin with their classroom design. Planning for the "average" and then adapting lessons to meet the needs of students in the margins, such as those with disabilities, who are gifted, or who are not native English speakers, was time-consuming and simply not working. Understanding this, the principal decided to explore the Universal Design for Learning (UDL) framework and, subsequently, to consider how to introduce UDL to her staff.

The school's administrative team knew they had to be strategic in presenting the UDL framework to teachers because of significant changes already occurring in their school relating to staffing and resources. The administrators did not want teachers to see UDL as "just one more thing" or another fad; thus they had to present it as "the way we do things here." The team's approach was to model the UDL framework through the design and implementation of professional development opportunities, which were a natural fit because of the variability of the teachers in the school.

"MUST HAVES": SHARED VISION, POSITIVE CULTURE, HIGH EXPECTATIONS

In 1932, sociologist Willard Waller (2014) stated, "Schools have a culture that is definitely their own. There are, in the school, complex rituals of personal relationships, a set of folkways, mores, and irrational sanctions, a moral code based upon them. There are traditions, and traditionalists waging their world-old battle against innovators" (p. 69). When a new administration joins a school, it sometimes meets resistance because it threatens to challenge traditions that have been in place for years and question a culture that has become so entrenched that the thought of change is terrifying.

Before a school community can come to value professional learning, certain foundational pillars need to be in place to ensure that a true transformation can occur and be sustained. These pillars include a shared vision; a healthy, thriving culture; strong relationships; clear expectations for all stakeholders; and putting value on professional learning. Each of these pillars builds on the others.

Developing a Shared Vision

Halstead Academy needed to begin with a shared vision because each teacher was working in isolation and the school community had no shared goals. The new administrative team inherited a leadership team with great variability, ranging from those with strong personalities, those who knew the history of the school, and those who were effective educators. At the first leadership meeting, the group began to discuss what they wanted for Halstead. The discussion revolved around how the team felt about the school, what they wanted the school to become, and what direction they wanted it to move in. Several teachers shared hopeful ideas about the school becoming a place that valued students and the community, a place with high expectations for its students, and a place that would help students succeed no matter their needs or circumstances. Mrs. W., a teacher who had been in the school for at least fifteen years, was on the leadership team. The faculty respected her and the community appreciated her, yet no one really knew how Mrs. W. viewed the school and its students until she chimed in during this conversation: "These ideas are great and everything, but it isn't like we are preparing these kids for Princeton." Her attitude was exactly the reason why establishing a vision, a mission, and core beliefs for the school were essential to creating a culture that would value professional learning and embrace the UDL framework.

To create a strong foundation, a school's teachers must reach consensus on several large issues: Why do we exist? What must our school become to accomplish our purpose? How must we behave to achieve our vision? How will we mark our progress? (DuFour, DuFour, Eaker, & Many, 2006). The question "Why do we exist?" is a good place to open the conversation about developing the school's mission or sense of purpose. Through such conversations, teachers and administrators can begin to learn about the staff's beliefs and educational philosophies, and determine whether they are on the same page. Our education system is designed around the idea that most people learn in similar ways and that "a fair education is an identical one" (Meyer, Rose, & Gordon, 2014). Thus, it was essential for the Halstead Academy leadership team to ensure that all faculty members would begin to see that the traditional conception of education could not meet the needs of all learners. A fair education system does not see all students as identical, and to meet the challenge of learner variability, the school community must share a belief in equity and high expectations for all learners.

Creating a Culture That Values Learner Variability

In October, the fifth-grade team requested that the principal of Halstead attend their next grade-level meeting. The principal was excited to be included in the group and looked forward to participating in some collaborative planning. Unfortunately, the team had a hidden agenda. The meeting began with a series of excuses as to why they were unable to teach their students: "These kids can't learn because…how can you expect us to teach when they can't…understand where our kids come from?"

Finally, the team brought up Shawn, a student with significant problem behavior who the team said was preventing his classmates from learning. The principal proposed several interventions, and each was met with, "That won't work because…" Ms. F. said, "You know what, I am done with Shawn. I am just going to focus on everyone else." The principal responded, "We are never done with kids. It is our job to figure out what we can change to make sure he is successful." The principal encouraged the team to create a plan for Shawn, a student in the margins, and suggested that they offer the supports they provided Shawn to the rest of the class as well. She was quietly laying a foundation for UDL, a framework in which planning for those in the margins works for all and that sees the curriculum as disabled, not the students. The principal realized that she needed to alter teachers' belief that students were "broken" or needed to change, and to shift their focus from changing the students to changing the environment.

The culture of a school is established through the core beliefs of the teachers, staff, and administration, such as the manner in which teachers interact or the pedagogy they use to deliver an instructional program. A school that encourages and promotes growth for all is one in which teachers have established a collaborative culture that eventually will evolve into a professional learning community. In sum, collaborating effectively is an essential component in building a community that values professional learning.

Another aspect that must be considered when attempting to create a culture that values professional learning is understanding and respecting the social environment of the students the school serves. When school staff understands the environment students come from and the challenges they encounter, they can create a teaching and learning culture that meets students where they are. As Novak (2014) states, we cannot fix the challenges our students bring to us, but we can fix the way we approach those challenges to ensure that all students learn: "If you remove the barriers in your learning environments, you take away many of the reasons and excuses for failure. Then, and only then, you can teach every student" (p. 13).

Cultivating High Expectations

Stephen Covey (2014) said, "Treat a man as he is and he will remain as he is. Treat a man as he can and should be and he will become as he can and should be." Such expectations drive a school's vision and culture. Once the school has created a vision and established a positive culture, high expectations must become the norm for the entire school community. Faculty, staff, students, and parents often expect the school administration to set expectations and hold everyone accountable for meeting them. That kind of top-down leadership is destined to fail, but when all stakeholders hold each other accountable for meeting expectations, the school belongs to everyone.

The UDL framework is based on the premise that we can engage all students in our classrooms. Novak (2014) notes that we cannot "prevent all of the challenges students will face, but we can alleviate them by designing a learning that leaves no room for failure.... [T]o do this, we need to be surrounded by people who have the same belief" (p. 3). At Halstead, the expectation soon became that teachers were committed to the school's vision and goals and that they would work together to create a culture grounded in high expectations. It was no longer was acceptable to believe that only some students, or only some teachers, could reach their goals.

Today at Halstead Academy, teachers are empowered to "drive the bus," but the administration provides the map. If a teacher does not embrace high expectations for all, other teachers are quick to remind them "how we do it here at Halstead." When new teachers join the staff, the veteran teachers model expectations. The staff provides support, guidance, and suggestions to these novices; however, they also can recognize an individual who is unwilling to live up to expectations. If a colleague does not believe that all students can become expert learners, the staff is empowered to have the difficult conversation as to whether that person has future at Halstead. Moreover, the staff has high expectations not only for students but for themselves as educators, and they are empowered to identify their own learning goals.

ESTABLISHING A CULTURE THAT VALUES PROFESSIONAL LEARNING

In the past, the teachers at Halstead were not receptive to new learning, nor did they understand the impact professional development and teacher collaboration could have on student achievement. To provide personalized educational experiences and facilitate change, the administration and instructional resource team established a professional learning community and designed a series of flexible, engaging professional development sessions that included lesson study, instructional rounds, and flexible options for professional learning time.

Lesson Study

Lesson study is an effective strategy that involves refining pedagogical practices and examining content standards. It provides opportunities for collaboration and reflective conversation among peers. These benefits are critical components of professional growth, which made lesson studies the logical starting point in establishing a manageable community of active adult learners at Halstead that also allowed teachers to understand the importance of change.

This process began with Halstead's fourth-grade team. While typically a learning experience for all, the main purpose in this case was to illustrate the need for a common vision, professional learning, and consistent expectations for teachers. This was an enlightening experience for two teachers in particular. After observing a peer teach an ineffective lesson that had been meticulously planned as a team, it was evident that not all classrooms were successfully implementing the curriculum, making responsive decisions, or creating an environment where students could feel safe and ready to learn. This professional experience was a catalyst for altering teachers' mindsets. However, designing a lesson that offered multiple means of engagement, representation, action, and expression was only one piece of the puzzle; delivering the lesson effectively was also fundamental. To help teachers make the shift from planning to implementation, the administrative team worked to identify structures that would enable teachers to see effective instruction in practice.

Instructional Rounds

Conducting instructional rounds, or "learning walks," is a longstanding practice that encourages teachers to observe best practices in action and to reflect on their own practice (City, Elmore, Fiarman, & Teitel, 2009). Like the lesson studies, the initial purpose of introducing rounds at Halstead was to give teachers perspective on their practice and the chance to look for patterns of improvement across the school. The administrative team initially chose to use classrooms as models of high-quality instruction, but many teachers objected because they felt that if their classroom was not chosen it reflected negatively on their practice. To foster a sense of community, the administrative team decided to open all classrooms to the instructional rounds, which also helped instill a sense of shared responsibility for the learning process.

As the instructional rounds process evolved, teachers began to identify specific areas of focus, such as application of the attributes of a twenty-first-century classroom that focuses on collaboration, creativity, communication, and critical thinking. Halstead also worked to align the Danielson Framework for Teaching and UDL with the school's overall plan, which identified instructional rounds as a way to measure progress. The purpose of each round is set before a visit and the norms are reviewed (Table 4.1). Each group visits four classrooms for approximately ten minutes, during which they collect evidence to support the targeted topic: the teacher's words and actions, students' words and actions, and classroom artifacts. The instructional round culminates in a reflection, first as individuals and then as a conversation among all participants. They focus on practices they observed that effectively support learner-centered, universally designed environments and discuss how these ideas can be embedded in all classrooms.

TABLE 4.1 Instructional rounds summary

INSTRUCTIONAL ROUNDS ARE...	INSTRUCTIONAL ROUNDS ARE NOT...
• Idea generators	• Evaluative
• About awareness	• Judgmental
• About rigor and relevance	• About critiquing
• About improving instructional practices and building competencies	
• About reflective practice	

Note: Instructional round norms were established with teachers and are reviewed prior to each learning walk. Following the experience we reflect on the norms to ensure we met the demands of the activity.

One of the greatest misconceptions about UDL is that it begins and ends with the lesson plan. Although it is important to apply the UDL framework to the lesson plan, it is most powerful when applied to the overall learning environment. Instructional rounds provide a platform for viewing the learning environment through a UDL lens. The Halstead leadership team distinguished three areas of focus during its instructional rounds: teacher, students, and space. These targets aligned with the district's shift toward student-centered learning, which has a foundation in the UDL framework (see Chapter 8, "Scaling the Work: A Small District Perspective"). Halstead also identified questions related to these targets that teachers can consider while visiting classrooms (see Figures 4.1 and 4.2).

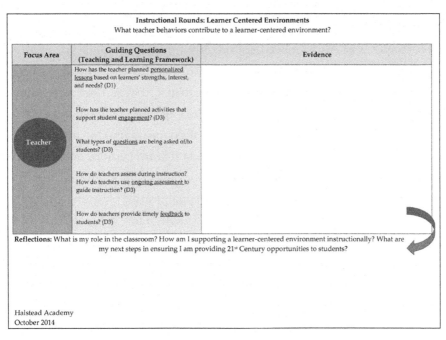

FIGURE 4.1 Instructional rounds rubrics

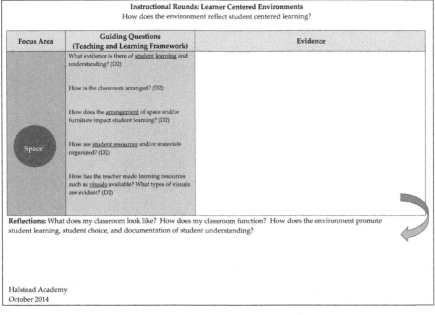

FIGURE 4.2 More instructional rounds rubrics

Professional Learning Time

Lesson studies and instructional rounds illuminated the need for change at Halstead and also demonstrated the importance of thoughtful, focused planning and ongoing collaboration. The district bargaining agreement requires teachers to have 250 minutes of planning time, which many used to run personal errands, while "collaboration" often meant making photocopies for each other. Few of the teachers' professional conversations actually centered on instructional practice or student achievement. It became clear to the administrative team that the staff needed a collaborative planning structure that specifically focused on student achievement. They also saw that they would have to delineate what should occur during professional learning time.

Through creative scheduling and budget adjustments, the administration was able to provide teachers with additional planning time each week, which was dedicated to professional conversations centered on student data and content standards. The grade-level teachers and all resource staff (reading specialist, instructional coach, math resource teacher) were present and were given a topic to focus on. All grade levels participated and the meeting was not optional; in fact, at first it was quite uncomfortable. But over time the educators developed common language, were given valuable resources, and began to build strong professional relationships—all of which were key steps in creating a culture that was ready to grow.

NEW OPPORTUNITIES FOR PROFESSIONAL LEARNING

Most administrators would agree that, after a long Monday of teaching and learning, the last thing teachers wanted was to attend an afterschool meeting. The Halstead administration observed that Monday faculty meetings often were attended by people with blank stares, or who were checking email and grading papers. Like any responsive practitioners, the administration reconsidered how to meet the needs of their "students"—the classroom teachers. They used their knowledge of adult learners to design professional learning opportunities that recognized the variability of the teachers. The new opportunities they offered included whole-group, small-group, and individualized professional development.

Whole Group

The leadership team understood that whole-group meetings were the least effective mode of professional development, but they also recognized that there were times when district expectations had to be communicated to all teachers. To disseminate this information in meaningful, engaging ways that deviated from the traditional faculty meeting, they looked at delivery options that used multiple means of representation. They decided to adopt a "flipped" classroom approach, and harnessed the power of digital media to provide teachers with resources to explore on their own. After reviewing resources such as videos, articles, or websites, teachers discussed how this information would impact their instruction and student achievement. Together they created multimedia projects that they used to communicate their new understandings to their colleagues.

The benefits of the flipped model were significant, the greatest being the teachers' ability to view the online resources on their own time. Teachers spent countless hours planning and preparing for their students, and they also actively collaborated to monitor and revise their own thinking. The flipped model enabled them to explore the new tools in order to present their learning—tools such as Padlet or Discovery Boards that may also be beneficial in the classroom. Most important, using the flipped classroom model to deliver instruction to the staff allowed them to experience multiple means of representation, action, and expression as learners. Modeling UDL in professional learning sessions is a powerful strategy that helps teachers see the benefits of using it in their own instruction.

Small Group

The Halstead leadership team worked diligently to find ways to customize and personalize professional learning for teachers. The team provided a full day of coverage to each grade level each month to allow teachers time to focus on topics and activities connected to the school's vision and its progress plan. This structure relied on the strength of the specialists in the school, including the reading specialist, special educators, and the math resource teacher. This provided varied perspectives and in turn set reflective practice in motion.

The typical components of the grade-level meetings are as follows:

Problems Seeking Solutions   Teachers voice their concerns in the form of a question to facilitate sharing ideas within the group.

Data Analysis   The team triangulates data and uses them to form small groups that customize instruction to meet the needs of students.

Professional Development   The instructional coach facilitates professional learning activities that meet the needs of each specific grade level.

Application and Responsive Planning   Teachers apply their new learning to content planning and/or activities in small groups.

In these sessions, teachers are encouraged to be expert learners, and they put multiple UDL guidelines into practice. The sessions foster community and collaboration among team members and allow the administration to provide mastery-oriented feedback relative to the school's goals. Productivity and collaboration are maximized through careful goal-setting and strategic planning. And again, the UDL framework is modeled in professional learning, with the idea that the teachers as learners will experience the power of the framework.

Individualized Professional Development

Finally, Halstead Academy has embraced opportunities for individualized professional development. To organize this movement and streamline many of the district initiatives and expectations, Halstead adopted the university model for organizing individualized professional development. Teachers begin the school year by reflecting on their instructional practices and professional needs using the Danielson framework, the school district's chosen evaluation tool. With the assistance of resource teachers and the administration, teachers identify their own goal, develop a plan to meet that goal, and identify how this goal will impact student achievement. Identifying the what, why, and how is another way to utilize the UDL framework in professional learning. Teacher goals are aligned to the elements of the Danielson framework and staff then use the adapted teacher development plan to support their model of professional learning (see Figure 4.3).

Teacher Professional Development Plan: Halstead Academy

Teacher _____ Grade Level _____

Based on your self-assessment, your administrator's input, and any school or district initiatives, what professional development goal have you identified? What is an area of knowledge or skill you would like to strengthen?

How does it relate to the domains and components of the BCPS evaluation criteria?

What would success on this goal look like? How will you know when you have achieved it? What would count as evidence of success?

Pre-Assessment	Post-Assessment

Adapted from: BCPS Department of Staff Relations and Employees Performance Management • Teacher Evaluation Teacher Development Plan • August 7, 2013

Describe the activities you will do to work toward your goal, and their anticipated timelines. Please refer to Halstead 2.0 for a list of options.			
Timeline	Activity	Point Value	Reflection Form Completed

What resources will you need to better achieve your goal?

This was discussed and agreed upon.

Teacher Signature _____ Date _____

Teacher Signature _____ Date _____

Adapted from: BCPS Department of Staff Relations and Employees Performance Management • Teacher Evaluation Teacher Development Plan • August 7, 2013

FIGURE 4.3 Teacher development plan

The teachers have access to a menu of professional development opportunities on the Halstead Academy 2.0 website (*www.tinyurl.com/halsteadacademy2*), which offers the requirements, expectations, and forms necessary to monitor their learning.

These options include:

Book Study   Teachers are grouped by common goals and facilitate a study on a book the group selects. The literature aligns to the desired professional outcome. A facilitator schedules meetings and develops essential questions for consideration. This experience culminates in a book review the group writes and presents to the rest of the faculty.

Coaching Session   The instructional coach can support each teacher by modeling, co-teaching, coaching, and providing feedback through the lens of the teacher's goal. This situational experience maximizes personalized and customized professional learning.

Presentation   Share the wealth—teachers often hoard their amazing ideas, but the experience of presenting allows teachers to share their *next* practices with their peers during whole-group time.

Article or Tutorial   Teachers who would like to share their new ideas as they pertain to their desired goal can do so in the form of an article or web tutorial (using screencast tools).

Learning Walk   Teachers observe several classrooms in the school building, looking for trends, effective practices, and student engagement. This experience culminates in a reflective, nonevaluative conversation with the instructional coach.

Lesson Study   Teachers again form groups based on similar goals or across grade levels. Together they plan a lesson using best practices, as cited in the current educational literature. One member implements the lesson while the rest of the group observes. Teachers then reflect on the lesson using formative assessments and observation tools connected to their goal. They then repeat the process, implementing changes they deem necessary to improve the lesson.

Peer Observation   Teachers observe a peer noted for strength in the area they wish to improve. For example, teachers working to identify best practices for their inclusive classroom would observe special educators.

Conference/Workshop/Webinar/Online Course   Often teachers engage in educational learning opportunities, such as workshops, webinars, and so forth, on their own, but they rarely reflect on or share this new learning with others. This experience allows teachers to engage in material aligned with their own goal, on their own time.

These options offer teachers ways to reach their desired goal and enable them to read, see, do, and reflect. Halstead 2.0 employs many UDL Guidelines, including offering options for recruiting interest (providing choice and autonomy), for expression and communication (using multiple tools for construction and composition), for sustaining effort and persistence (fostering community and collaboration), and for supporting executive functions (guiding goal-setting and supporting planning and strategy development). These individual professional learning experiences are made more powerful because the district itself is engaged in a shift to a student-centered environment. What better way to learn to create a student-centered, universally designed environment than to experience it as a learner yourself?

What New Opportunities for Professional Learning Look Like

In committing to the learner-centered movement, Halstead Academy and the school district have adopted a 1:1 initiative to give students opportunities to engage in twenty-first-century learning experiences. This can be a daunting task for any teacher, but it was particularly so for Mrs. K., one of Halstead's kindergarten teachers, who asked, "What am I supposed to do with these devices with five-year-olds?" It was clear this teacher would be considering the question for the remainder of the school year, both consciously and subconsciously. The administrative team encouraged her to use the question to guide her professional learning.

Using the Halstead 2.0 menu, Mrs. K. decided to participate in a book group about digital learning using *Amplify* by Katie Muhtaris and Kristen Zemke (2015). The teachers could move through the book at their own pace, reflect on their practices, and ask each other questions about next practices. This promoted collaboration and communication between teachers at multiple grade levels, and prompted the quiet leaders of the school to emerge as vocal trailblazers while embracing the role of facilitator.

Mrs. K. also sought out teachers in the building who were emerging as leaders in integrating technology in their instruction. Using a peer observation template (Figure 4.4), Mrs. K. could document meaningful practices as they were implemented. Afterward she met with her colleagues to reflect on their planning, implementation, and the overall impact on student learning.

Finally, Mrs. K. participated in a lesson study, which encouraged a small group of teachers to craft lessons collaboratively using what they knew about pedagogy, student development, and grade-level standards. Each teacher had the opportunity to present the lesson to their class while their colleagues observed, after which they reflected on the lesson and made changes that would maximize student achievement. This practice truly put theory into practice and is a model of universally designed professional learning that includes both choice and voice. This university model has helped to build a community of collaborators, fostered reflective practice, and encouraged teachers to emerge as leaders. It values the individual goals of each professional and offers a personalized pathway to reach these goals. It also allows teachers to experience multiple options and pathways in their own learning.

Peer Observation

Topic: Working with Special Needs
Date and Time: Tuesday, March 15 from 9:00–10:15

Focus	Observations/Questions
Visual Supports What visual supports does the teacher provide to the sudent? How do the visuals support the needs of the students?	
Behavioral Supports What behavioral supports does the teacher provide to the sudent? How are the supports presented to students? How do supports impact student performance, behavior, and/or focus?	
Teacher Language What is the tone of the teacher? How does the teacher speak to the students when redirecting? How does the teacher communicate expectations?	

FIGURE 4.4 Peer observation template

CONCLUSION

Establishing a community that values professional learning does not happen overnight; like UDL, it is an iterative process of change. A strong and thriving professional learning community developed at Halstead Academy as a result of rethinking professional learning and modeling options for representation, action, and expression. Moreover, by engaging the staff in setting a vision and building the school culture, expectations for teaching and learning were thoughtfully developed, based on shared goals. Teachers and leaders who became engaged in their own learning changed the direction of the school, which has had a positive impact on student achievement by building a culture based on high expectations for all learners, teachers and students alike.

5

Building a UDL Culture: Professional Learning Communities

Nicole Norris

GUIDING QUESTION

- As a leader or member of a school community, how do you provide the environment, the professional development, and the time for school staff to change their mindset, learn about, and embrace Universal Design for Learning (UDL)?

This chapter, which is narrated in the voice of a middle school principal, offers insights into the journey of a school staff from first becoming aware of Universal Design for Learning, then through the learning process, and on to its implementation. Building a UDL culture at Lansdowne Middle School (LMS) began with forming a small professional learning community (PLC), whose members recognized the need for change, had the desire to learn, and made a commitment to their personal professional growth. Forming this UDL PLC led to the creation of learning opportunities for students and professional development opportunities for the school staff. The PLC membership, which grew each year, included both long-time staff members and some new to the school. The administration made important decisions when selecting members and implementing the PLC, and provided specific supports and incentives for the teachers to join. Among the many lessons learned were how to build interest in and motivation for professional learning, the role the administration should play in supporting the PLC, the need to assess strategies and barriers throughout the implementation of UDL, and how important professional development and mindset were to sustaining a UDL culture.

INTRODUCTION

Many terms were used to describe Lansdowne Middle School (LMS): the highest poverty middle school in our district, a Tier III school, a Title I school, highly diverse, urban/suburban, restructured…definitely challenging. None of these terms would make you think that a dedicated staff was at work inside this windowless brick building, each day showing their dedication, caring, and commitment to their students' learning and growth. The school culture reflected the school motto, "Believe and Achieve." The teachers were there every day, making safety, learning, communication, and collaboration a top priority. When the administration decided to introduce UDL, it was taking the risk that a small group of educators would be willing to reflect deeply on their individual practices, openly engage in conversation about removing existing barriers to effective learning, and make a commitment to their own professional growth.

UDL is a framework based on scientific insights into how humans learn (Meyer, Rose, & Gordon, 2014), which was developed as a method for improving and optimizing teaching and learning for all people. The UDL framework gave educators at LMS a structure that enabled them to design flexible learning environments that would meet the needs of a wide range of learners. The process began with a small group of educators who decided to embrace the UDL Guidelines because they believed it could be the way to connect the school's various initiatives. Something magical happened as we began the UDL journey at LMS—the more we learned, the more we wanted to know, and the more we wanted to share. Once it started, it couldn't be stopped.

BUILDING INTEREST AND MOTIVATION FOR PROFESSIONAL LEARNING

Many school leaders have experience rolling out multiple district initiatives and individual school initiatives at the same time. This can be overwhelming to staff, and they often lose the focus. When introducing new conceptions through a PLC, it is extremely important to set the stage by recruiting adult learners who will motivate others, and who have the desire to provide not only new learning opportunities to their students but also professional development opportunities for their colleagues. Participating in a PLC should not feel like work; it should ignite passion for the profession (Novak, 2014). Staff members participating in a PLC must be comfortable and confident when engaging in challenging conversations because such discussions have the potential to alter mindsets and produce significant changes in how the school community experiences teaching and learning.

At LMS, the more we explored UDL and the more we learned from other districts and colleagues who were implementing the framework, the more we knew it was what our school needed to help spark a connection and promote a common language among the multiple initiatives going on in our fast-paced school. We knew that our staff needed UDL, but more importantly that this common instructional language would help us address learner variability, which our students definitely needed. The language of the UDL Guidelines, our access to low- and high-tech tools, and being able to recognize some current practices within the Guidelines were reassuring and motivating to our PLC, which made this journey exciting and extremely worthwhile.

Our introduction to UDL began with participation in a UDL professional learning experience led by CAST and funded by the Bill & Melinda Gates Foundation (CAST, 2012a) (*www.udlcenter.org/implementation/fourdistricts*). We were fortunate to be one of two middle schools (out of 175 schools in our district) that were involved in this project. Our district had provided various professional development opportunities on UDL over the years, but it never took hold enough to impact our curriculum design and instructional decision making. The purpose of this project was to explore and pilot processes and tools to support UDL implementation within our district.

To kick off the project, we decided to introduce the UDL framework to the instructional leadership team. This was done for two reasons: (1) to educate all department chairs, physical education and fine arts included, on a new way of learning that their department members might want to engage in, and (2) to pique school leaders' interest in UDL as a way to build their capacity to reach all learners and motivate their department teams. Each department chair built a strong relationship with their department members and engaged in many conversations about expectations for effective instruction. Fortunately, two instructional leaders at LMS were extremely interested in becoming members of the PLC after hearing a presentation on the foundations of UDL. Their interest stemmed from wanting to remove barriers and provide instruction that was accessible to all students. Being teachers in a school and a community where they had to earn the respect of their students and during a time of high accountability, the idea of removing barriers and providing more access and opportunity for students was hopeful and exciting.

Our work progressed rapidly after the leadership information session. We decided that one member from each department should participate in the UDL PLC. The two instructional leaders, in consultation with the administration, selected teachers from each content area to join the PLC; this was a departure from the past, when teachers often could choose to join a project rather than waiting to be selected. The teachers were chosen carefully, with consideration given to those who were team players, showed their interest in professional growth, persevered in their work, and would be open to taking risks and engaging in deep instructional conversations. Seven educators from seven different content areas agreed to join the PLC. At that moment, we did not realize the huge impact these choices would have in moving the work forward.

To prepare for the work of the UDL PLC, these seven teachers and their department chairs engaged in a two-day workshop on UDL. It was important for the department chairs to participate alongside the teachers to ensure that all staff were receiving the same message. For most who attended, this workshop was their first introduction to UDL. It included a balance of direct instruction, exploration, resource review, collaboration, and goal-setting, which taught the team the basics of UDL and built their excitement about the journey.

> *The biggest shift in my practice was to make the learning process explicit for students. Before learning about UDL, I approached teaching like a magician approaches a magic show. I planned lessons that helped students meet the objective, but the students never knew how I performed the tricks behind the learning. Now that I base my lessons on the UDL Guidelines, I focus on helping my students become expert learners. I help my students determine how they learn best, set goals, and create a plan to reach those goals. I give them the power to direct their own learning while explicitly teaching them how to use strategies to navigate the learning process. Students are still learning content, but now they are also learning how to learn. I hope that they are able to use their skills to succeed outside the controlled environment of my classroom and the school building.*
>
> —AMANDA HUGHES, Language Arts Department Chair, LMS

COLLABORATION AND COMMUNICATION

Collaboration and communication have to be a top priority of a PLC. Team members must be aware of one another's strengths and needs, and it is critical that they create an environment in which all participants' thoughts and opinions are heard, valued, and respected. Creating this culture at LMS took time, patience, and honest conversation.

Our PLC training began with an activity that required participants to plan a collaborative lesson on UDL Exchange (*udlexchange.cast.org*). This proved to be more of a challenge than any member thought it would be, but it also gave the team a chance to learn how to work together and to give each other honest feedback. Scaffolds and supports were built into the lesson-planning format to provide assistance when needed, and we were fortunate to have the support of three facilitators who took on different roles throughout the implementation process. One facilitator served as our UDL expert, one assisted with lesson planning and the UDL implementation, and one supported the integration of technology by helping teachers access low- and high-tech resources.

The facilitators were critical to our UDL PLC's success: they supported the teachers with their understanding of UDL and eventually built an independent support system within the school, which they did using a coaching model. At first the facilitators were available to assist with UDL planning only every two weeks, but they were reachable by phone and email and were willing to answer questions and help with any challenges and barriers raised by the PLC members. During visits to the school, the facilitators met with teachers during planning periods to discuss how to integrate UDL and new technology into their lessons, to observe lessons they were invited to attend, and to listen to the needs of the PLC members. The teachers greatly appreciated this support, which helped them change their mindsets and some of their practices. The facilitators also held monthly UDL PLC meetings that focused on the needs of the PLC members.

The facilitators' support helped the PLC members build confidence in their understanding of the UDL Guidelines, in integrating UDL into one lesson each week, and in their conversations about instructional practices. The facilitators also gave teachers the support they needed to take the risk of implementing the UDL framework. This allowed them to make mistakes in their planning and implementation while having time for reflection, which helped the teachers grow professionally. After taking such risks, a teacher could debrief with the facilitator to discuss what went well, what needed to change, how they had implemented UDL during the lesson, and what impact it had. Because the PLC members included teachers from almost every school department, these instructional conversations started to spread, and teachers not involved in the UDL PLC became curious about the training the group was receiving and the work they were doing.

> *Developing a PLC that is focused on UDL has helped me see that strategic, purposeful planning benefits all students when we consider learner variability at every step.*
>
> —KATHY KELBAUGH, STAT teacher, PBE

THE ROLE OF ADMINISTRATION IN BUILDING A PLC

It is extremely important that the administrator responsible for starting a PLC engage in the learning with their team. It is their responsibility to help set the goals for professional growth and highlight the benefits of being a PLC member. They also must purposefully decide who will lead the PLC and allow the leader to invite colleagues they recognize as influential members of the school staff to join. Although not all members will evaluate others, they must be strong enough to give their colleagues feedback and be comfortable hosting learning walks in their classrooms.

At the start of this project I was familiar with UDL, but it was not information I could share with others or teach others to implement. I therefore decided to attend all the UDL professional development sessions to build my own knowledge so I could both offer support and grow professionally with the PLC. This may have been the best decision that I made during the UDL journey. It was evident to me early on that UDL was a framework that all other school initiatives could fall under. All programs, curricular changes, and instructional expectations could be tied to the Guidelines and to the purpose of providing access to learning for all students. The staff needed to sense my passion about learning that could alter instructional practices and mindsets throughout our school.

As mentioned earlier, two members of our UDL PLC were also part of our instructional leadership team, which was beneficial in that the PLC's learning and progress could be discussed in our weekly leadership meetings. This encouraged other team members to learn more about UDL, to use the resources the PLC members were using in their own instruction, and to talk about the UDL Guidelines with their department members during co-planning and department meetings. Thus the leadership team began to share ideas and strategies they had tried themselves or had observed one of their department members using. As a result, the expectations of what effective instruction looked like started to change, and the leadership team began to use the UDL Guidelines to establish "look-fors" during informal and formal classroom observations.

The PLC focus on using the UDL Guidelines in planning sessions extended to the instructional leadership team, which helped move our work from preparing to integrating the UDL implementation process (Figure 5.1). Each PLC member approached these phases in different ways, but the more we used the Guidelines in our planning and observed effective instruction through that lens, the faster our work moved forward. It was extremely important that our UDL PLC shared their new knowledge of UDL with the rest of the staff and provided examples of how they integrated it into their instruction. The professional development sessions our PLC presented were powerful proof of the success they were experiencing by taking a new approach to planning that included the mindset that LMS could provide access to instruction for every student in our school.

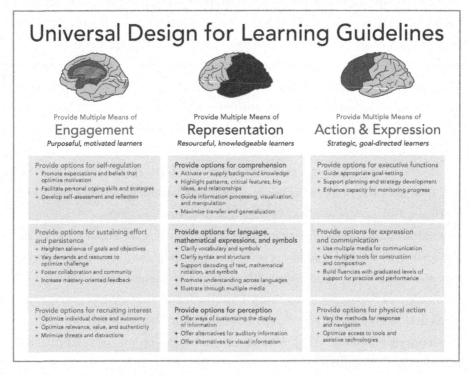

FIGURE 5.1 The UDL Guidelines © CAST 2014. USED WITH PERMISSION.

About eighteen months into the UDL PLC implementation, we had huge turnover on the instructional leadership team. Five new department chairs, four who were also new to the school, became members of the team. At that time we also began an exciting new district initiative that allowed secondary schools to hire a full-time teacher dedicated to professional development, which is a catalyst for changing instructional practices. Fortunately, two members of the instructional leadership team were also members of the PLC, and thus were instrumental in helping the administration bring the new department chairs up to speed on UDL. They could explore, understand, and eventually use the UDL Guidelines in their own instruction, with the assistance of the PLC members and one of the facilitators. They soon could to observe instruction and provide feedback through a UDL lens, although this was initially somewhat challenging—some department members knew more about UDL than their new department chairs, which made the teachers and the new chairs somewhat uncomfortable. But with support from the leadership team and the facilitators, the new chairs worked to integrate UDL into their lessons, into their departmental professional development, and into instructional conversations with their department members. They used this as a learning opportunity for the entire staff. Eventually they conducted learning walks between departments and used UDL to guide their observations and instructional conversations (CAST, 2012b).

As our understanding of UDL improved and its use became more integrated, various other district initiatives began to change. For example, we began to use the Danielson Framework for Teaching (CAST, 2012c) as our evaluation tool. It was extremely important to me that teachers could connect the UDL Guidelines with this new tool, and that they were communicated in a way that would enable teachers to see that proper UDL implementation would likely lead to high ratings during formal observations. For example, Domain 3 of the Danielson Framework for Teaching states, "Instructional materials and resources are suitable to the instructional purposes and engage students mentally. Students initiate the choice, adaptation, or creation of materials to enhance their learning." All of our professional development sessions began by connecting the teachers' new learning to both the Danielson Framework for Teaching and the UDL Guidelines, since it was important that instructional feedback from the administration and department chairs and from our professional development teacher was in a common language that incorporated both of these elements.

The leadership team was able to communicate clear expectations about effective instruction to the staff, provide meaningful professional development to support these expectations, and assess and respond to teachers' needs. As an administrator during this process, I learned to be a better listener because my mindset allowed me to engage in deep reflection and conversation about instruction, teaching, and learning, and how that could lead to my own growth and the growth of the students and staff. I had made a commitment to learn about UDL, which enabled me to listen to what the other PLC members were learning and to understand how they were translating the framework into meaningful instruction. I could sense when they were confused or challenged, or when they became overly excited that the Guidelines were giving their students new avenues to access and engage with instruction. I also gave them the flexibility to take risks, to reflect on the results, and to use these risky opportunities to improve their students' learning.

> *For me, UDL just doesn't begin in the classroom—it begins in my mind and how I think about teaching my lessons. UDL has changed how I view teaching, which in turn changes the way I deliver my lessons. As my mindset began to change, I was better prepared to meet the needs of all my learners. This is in fact at the very heart of what Universal Design for Learning is all about. We as educators need to make sure that we are reaching all of our learners and not just most. One way to accomplish this goal is to have our lessons prepared with diverse options for our students so they have the option to choose which assignment they want to do, enabling them to succeed! When we eliminate the one-size-fits-all mentality in our classroom instruction, we open the door of opportunity to reach all of our students. Our students come to us with diverse needs and learning styles, and we as educators need to be prepared to meet the diverse needs of our learners through instruction that engages our students, represents the materials in different ways, and allows them to express their learning in different ways.*
>
> —LAUREN KIMBLE, ESOL teacher, LMS

MONTHLY PLC MEETINGS

PLC meetings should be held monthly with a clear, specific agenda that outlines what will be accomplished. The expected outcomes should be communicated and proper resources provided. Teachers should engage in face-to-face learning for ninety minutes each month, but the learning should continue from meeting to meeting through conversations, learning walks, professional development presentations, and an online platform such as UDL Connect (*http://community.udlcenter.org/*).

The PLC at LMS often engaged in conversations about implementing UDL in lesson planning. Diving into deeper, honest conversations was tough at first because the group had never worked so closely together on a project and they needed time to get to know and trust one another. The agenda needed to include opportunities to discuss successes and challenges, to share information about lesson implementation, to plan, and to set deadlines and goals for future meetings. Deliverables were expected from each meeting, as was an action the group would reflect on using their online platform or at the next PLC meeting. An example of setting goals at an early UDL PLC meeting is found in Table 5.1.

TABLE 5.1 Summer professional development goals for UDL PLC

TIMELINE	GOAL
By the end of the summer	The PLC will be able to create and upload on UDL Exchange one collaborative lesson and one individual lesson, or a resource for a team-building activity.
By winter break	All departments will be introduced to UDL Exchange and the UDL Guidelines through presentations in department meetings.
By winter break	All PLC members will need to create and upload one lesson/resource in their content area on UDL Exchange.
By the end of the school year	PLC members will observe at least one PLC member and co-plan a cross-curricular UDL lesson and upload it on UDL Exchange.

Our UDL PLC members were thoughtful about the goals they created. They wanted to make sure they were reasonable and could be achieved within the time scheduled. The face-to-face meetings provided an opportunity for PLC members to measure their growth, to ask questions about the goals they had set, and to revise the goals if needed.

In the explore and prepare stages of the implementation process, our PLC experienced confusion, anxiety, and some frustration because they wanted to make sure they were understanding UDL and using it appropriately in planning. At this stage, it was important that they had conversations with one another, received reassurance and support from the facilitators, and could ask questions and bounce ideas off the administration about their instructional decisions. This deep reflection on instruction helped them achieve the mindset needed to properly implement and teach others about the UDL implementation process.

Our PLC members were consistently engaged in the ongoing learning that occurred during the UDL PLC meetings, due to our facilitators' thoughtful planning. It was important that these meetings were well planned and that the UDL Guidelines were used while they were being implemented. During the meetings teachers often learned something new about UDL, reflected on current practices and implementation of the UDL lesson, and learned about each other as educators and learners. Two particular learning opportunities our teachers experienced stand out for me because they generated meaningful discussion. One lesson had the teachers create their own formative assessment tool, which they would use when participating in UDL learning walks in our school, and the other asked teachers to participate in a scavenger hunt in the school environment. Having the teachers create their own formative assessment tool gave them a sense of ownership because they helped set the expectations for the observation process. It also reduced their anxiety; they knew exactly what evaluators would be looking for during observations and learning walks. During the scavenger hunt, the teachers went on learning walks without students and recorded evidence of UDL they observed in use in the school environment. After this activity, the PLC began to have conversations about their team members' individual strengths and needs, and discussed how they could provide executive function support to those who needed help organizing and arranging their classrooms. This also reiterated the importance of using the UDL Guidelines as a tool when making decisions to support student learning.

A major strength of our UDL PLC was that the group reflected on their practice and wanted to learn how to improve it, and were comfortable asking for and accepting assistance when needed. The climate of the PLC meetings gave them freedom to be honest with one another, and to ask the administration for help throughout the project. The meetings also enabled the members to be comfortable making recommendations and providing materials that were needed to continue the work through the following year. The recommendations included:

- Create a master schedule of "free space" and allow teachers to sign up to use empty classrooms, the gym, or the halls as flexible work spaces

- Provide ceiling mountings for the projectors

- Offer executive function assistance for teachers who need help organizing and arranging classrooms

- Visit other schools to see what they do with the physical space and furniture

Materials needed for the following year included:

- Folders and notebooks to keep in classrooms to help with student organization

- Bins for organization

- Magnets to turn chalkboards into manipulative stations

- Tape to transform floors into learning spaces

- Quick-response sleeves to reduce paper use

- Mini-whiteboards and more colored whiteboard markers

Members of the PLC noticed that, as new members joined and the work began to expand, the students began to change. The first noticeable change was their level of engagement with lessons. As teachers began to use the UDL Guidelines to plan and implement instruction, the students became excited about learning. Our PLC offered students more opportunities for group work, and provided movement, choice, and self-reflection that was not consistently offered in previous instruction. The work of the PLC included discussing and sharing ideas about how to give students more options for representation, as well as for action and expression. Students were given more responsibility to engage in learning, to teach one another, and to make choices about how this would occur. Over time, the students began to expect to be given these responsibilities, and they were frustrated when they had a substitute teacher or one who was not providing strong learning opportunities. The PLC meetings now included powerful discussions that centered around the change in students, since our teachers knew they were making a difference. The student outcomes provided clear evidence that this type of instruction was needed in every classroom, from every teacher, and the PLC members were eager to help other teachers make a difference for their students. The UDL implementation and learning were as exciting for the teachers as for the students.

STRATEGIES AND BARRIERS

When doing the work of a PLC, all members must be clear that there will be successes and challenges. Articulating the barriers is the best way for a PLC to assess their work and adjust so they can move forward. When doing so, it is extremely important that members are honest about their contributions to the PLC and reflect on their own learning and implementation of the Guidelines.

Our PLC often discussed what was working and what was not, which enabled them to acknowledge successes and address how to remove barriers. This reflection occurred often throughout the first year of UDL implementation, and was continued in the UDL PLC meetings. Examples of the strategies and barriers faced during our first year can be found in Table 5.2, and an example of the processing of strengths, weaknesses, opportunities, and threats during our second year can be found in Table 5.3.

TABLE 5.2 First-year strategies and barriers

STRATEGIES	BARRIERS
UDL PLC—choosing the right people at the right time	Initial anxiety and fears
Receiving monitoring and assistance from the facilitators provided time needed for focus and organization	Time needed to plan
Having access to technology and knowing which resources were available through the district—high tech and low tech	Time needed to experiment with planning resources
Deliverables were an expectation of UDL PLC monthly meetings	Overwhelmed with the number of resources
Holding PLC meetings and monthly meetings with district-level administrators	Questioning current practices and strategies—UDL implementation needed in more lessons
Accessing UDL Exchange and UDL Studio and sharing resources	Providing time and help for students to engage in self-reflection
Willingness of the PLC to share ideas through collaboration, professional development, and presentations	Allowing proper student processing time without stepping in Teacher mindset (outside of the PLC) Teacher capacity/time for PD

TABLE 5.3 Second-year strengths, weaknesses, opportunities, and threats

STRENGTHS—WHAT ARE OUR STRENGTHS THAT SUPPORT UDL?	• Biweekly PLC meetings • Three-credit CPD course • Support from facilitators • Just-in-time planning support for small group and technology integration • Technology enhances • Summer 3-Day UDL Institute at Towson University • UDL as a way to achieve "highly effective" in new evaluation system • Knowing what resources are available from the district, connecting them to the new evaluation, Common Core, and UDL—making deliberate connections • Focus on UDL and the learning environment • Focus on student-centered learning • Continuous reflection on UDL implementation • Young staff • Funds • Willingness to adapt • Flexibility • Many teachers willing to help one another and open classrooms to each other • Many teachers go above and beyond in supporting students

WEAKNESSES—WHAT DO WE NEED TO ADDRESS?	• Need to work as a whole faculty • Negative attitudes • Student stereotyping • Lack of technology at home • Little prior knowledge of technology • Lack of planning time • Lack of parent/student understanding
OPPORTUNITIES—WHAT OPPORTUNITIES DOES UDL IMPLEMENTATION OFFER?	• Increased learning for *all* students • More excitement about learning • Improved behavior • Choice
THREATS—WHAT THREATS NEGATIVELY IMPACT UDL IMPLEMENTATION?	• Teachers unwilling to embrace technology and jump into the 21st century • Not covering the entire curriculum • Time-consuming lessons • Wireless connection is suspect • Lack of natural light in school building • Inadequate skill set • Minds closed to change • Labeling students

Close analysis of these strategies, successes, and barriers helped our PLC grow, as the members celebrated what was working and to change what was not. The supports and resources they were given by the facilitators and the administration enabled them to continue to reflect and grow. They also were offered opportunities to communicate with one another, and to showcase their accomplishments and their professional growth.

> *UDL has completely changed my mindset about teaching. It challenges the educator to think, "Why does it have to be this way?" UDL challenges even the most mundane routines and forces you to think it through to ensure that all students will have access. If you do not think that the students will have equal access, then you know it needs some adjustment. I think it's important for the educator to step outside of their comfort zone to ensure equal access for all students. It provides an effective model for the students, especially because much of education is about having our students put themselves into uncomfortable situations/experiences. UDL provides a 3D education because it not only forces the educator to think about content, but it also encourages the student to develop executive function skills that are often lacking. I could not imagine teaching without UDL!*
>
> —ASHLEY LINK, seventh-grade world cultures teacher, LMS

UDL PLC AND PROFESSIONAL DEVELOPMENT

The work of a PLC can enhance the professional development a school offers its staff because the teachers invested in the work will share what they have learned—in our case, how UDL has changed their lesson-planning and implementation practices. With this focus on UDL, it is important that the professional development offered mirrors the practices expected in the classroom under the UDL implementation. The administration must use the UDL Guidelines to plan engaging professional development that offers multiple means of representation, and of action and expression. They must acknowledge, recognize, and plan for the variability that exists among the adult learners on their staff.

As soon as the LMS PLC began learning about UDL, they were willing to create professional development that would enable the entire school staff to begin using the UDL Guidelines to analyze their practices and recognize learner variability. The administration's role in professional development was to help establish the desired outcomes, help connect new learning to the school's evaluation system, and hand over ownership of the professional development to the PLC.

Learning from their peers that UDL could be the umbrella that would connect all other school initiatives was a powerful experience for our staff. The initial UDL PLC meetings often included discussion about the question, "What does UDL look like?" Our facilitators were hesitant to provide only a few examples, since the group might then believe what they saw was the only interpretation of UDL. At that moment we needed modeling, but it had to be authentic and unique.

> *UDL has had a huge impact on my mindset and instructional practices. I now realize that the most important thing I can teach my students is to learn to be learners. By offering them choices, they are not only more engaged in the instructional process but they are discovering how they learn best and how to be responsible learners, which will benefit them throughout their educational career. I have also realized that UDL does not require doing something huge. It is little things (i.e., visuals for vocabulary) that make a big difference. In reading, I have seen the huge impact that a literacy trekker can make on a student's comprehension of a text. Literacy trekkers have made my reading class more engaging and have increased students' levels of understanding.*
>
> —REBECCA OLINGER, second-grade teacher, PBE

One of our most meaningful professional development sessions took place early in the first year of the project. Our physical education teacher was excited about a lesson she had planned using the UDL Guidelines. She had spent a lot of time creating multiple means of action and expression and of representation for her students. This was an excellent lesson because it was connected to the content standards and provided low-tech and high-tech options, collaboration, specific directions, and checklists for self-reflection, and it used small groups through stations. On our professional development day, our teachers were asked to report to school in their workout gear so they could participate in the PE lesson. Afterward they were asked to work in teams to analyze the lesson using the UDL Guidelines, discuss what they learned, and determine how they could incorporate some of the PE teacher's ideas in their instruction. It was a hit!

During our second year of implementation, the school's UDL focus began to shift to the learning environment. Fortunately, our district began at the same time to provide professional development on student-centered learning focused on teacher, space, and students, which helped us create seamless connections between district initiatives, school initiatives, and our UDL implementation. Due to this marriage, the work we had started with UDL began to move from integration to scale, and this did not occur only through members of our UDL PLC.

We were fortunate to have made many professional contacts through the CAST/Gates grant project, and our partnership with Towson University and the Kennedy Krieger Institute. These connections continued to grow stronger, which allowed us to share more of our UDL work. These contacts gave our teachers numerous opportunities to provide ongoing professional development, not only to our staff but to several audiences outside the school. Several of our PLC members were asked to present at state and national professional conferences, they hosted a variety of visitors at our school, and their instruction was recorded for the UDL Implementation Series. I was fortunate to be able to share our UDL implementation journey with many audiences as well. These new and exciting opportunities helped us reflect on our work, set goals as a PLC, and make progress in strengthening our instructional practices. Teachers who were new to our building wanted to learn more about UDL implementation, and they were given feedback that helped them incorporate the UDL Guidelines into their instruction.

By the third year of UDL implementation, our staff had become comfortable hosting learning walks for one another, for other schools in our district, and eventually for school staff and district leaders from several other states. Each learning walk ended with a debriefing session, where all teachers who had been observed and all members of the UDL PLC and the leadership team were invited to share their observations. These conversations motivated the teachers because they were commended for their instruction, and they were eager both to answer questions and ask questions of our visitors. Although the visits could be a bit stressful, we always felt invigorated after sharing our learning and our story.

Consistent use of the UDL Guidelines while planning professional development was an expectation that carried through my time at LMS, and it was enhanced by presentations made by the professional development teacher and UDL PLC members during staff meetings. The need for a differentiated approach to professional development changed the focus of professional learning at our school, and UDL was used to meet the needs of our adult learners. When I took a new job as an elementary school principal, I was able to reflect on the UDL implementation process and the professional development at LMS, and to bring new understanding of the UDL Guidelines to the teachers at Prettyboy Elementary (PBE).

The PBE staff had learned about UDL and student-centered learning with their former principal, and they were comfortable engaging in reflective conversations about their instruction. Many of the teachers had in fact implemented the UDL Guidelines in their daily instruction, but they were not aware that their practices reflected this use. This connection became clear when they participated in a book study of UDL Now by Katie Novak, which focused on first understanding and then applying the UDL Guidelines.

Although the UDL implementation was in the explore and prepare phases when I arrived at PBE, the teachers were open to learning about the Guidelines, recognized them in their instruction, and soon began to use the Guidelines through choice assignments and literacy trekkers, which they had learned to do by reading UDL Now. The PBE fourth- and fifth-grade teachers also engaged in a professional development session that enabled them to learn about and plan for integrating UDL into their planning. Connecting with experts in the field, both face-to-face and virtually, is another way to support professional learning. If your school is not able to support a face-to-face session, there are many other ways to connect with leaders in the UDL field, such as Twitter, CAST webinars, and UDL Connect.

Those at the beginning of their UDL implementation journey may find the reflections of the PBE teachers useful. A simple way to begin the journey is to participate in a book study, which quickly helped teachers at PBE recognize that UDL could have a meaningful impact on their practices. The teachers offered the following reflections on what they were learning about UDL:

- Get your students involved by offering choices and providing opportunities for self-reflection.

- Provide opportunities for students to reflect on their own learning so that over time they can begin to see for themselves what type of learner they are. This, in turn, will help them make the best choices when you provide them choices in their learning.

- Observe students when you offer choice, and make choices available to *all* students.

- Scaffolding leads to success for all.

- Keep in mind the barriers to instruction and think of multiple ways you can remove them.

- Effective teacher planning allows for enhanced student learning and understanding.

- UDL is not one thing; it is many little things we do for students that make a big difference.

We will continue our professional development at PBE and use the UDL Guidelines to help us focus on responsive, small-group instruction that integrates the use of technology, scaffolding, choice, and a variety of resources. It is important that all educators at all grade levels explore and implement UDL. It is also essential for school leadership to provide professional learning options in all phases of UDL implementation: explore, prepare, integrate, scale, and optimize. Like our students, there is great variability among our staff members, and we need to ensure that professional learning options address this variability.

INCENTIVES AND CELEBRATIONS

Articulating the incentives for participating in a PLC is important, but not as important as choosing the right people at the right time. Although incentives are not mandatory, they do help recognize the PLC members' investment of time and hard work. Staff members who are committed to professional growth will not need monetary incentives to engage in meaningful work that will improve their instructional practices.

At LMS, we were fortunate to have the funds to give teachers a stipend for their participation in the UDL PLC, and they were also awarded continuing professional development credits for completing yearly requirements. Other incentives that we offered to motivate staff included:

- Attending professional conferences

- Presenting the work of the PLC at professional conferences

- Providing dedicated time for instructional conversations

- Providing coverage to engage in learning walks/debrief sessions

- Presenting at professional development sessions (we also provided time to plan)

- Presenting work of the PLC to district-level administrators

- Continuing professional development credit (in our district, this is associated with an increase in salary)

The teachers at LMS were excited to share their work and to network with others around the country about their UDL implementation journeys. Engaging in this work changed their mindsets and their beliefs about teaching and learning. They continue to provide access to learning for all students and to recognize and plan for barriers that are impeding student performance. They are an amazing group of educators, and I feel fortunate to know them and to continue to learn with them during our ongoing journey.

> *Prior to learning about UDL I would plan lessons thinking about my personal experiences and what I liked in as a student, and then I would get frustrated/annoyed when it didn't go as well as planned or students were not at the level I felt like they should be. With UDL I think more about my students and less about me. I think of the activities and then think of specific students. The thought process becomes is "Joe" going to do this? If not, what do I need to do to make the activity engaging to him while still meeting the objective? I do that for several kids and then in the end I am pretty confident that I have accounted for all types of learners and have planned ways to adjust the activity to have them be successful. For a long time I wanted to adjust the kids because it couldn't be my lesson or me that was causing the problem.*
>
> *UDL has helped my teaching become clearer. For example, I used to give kids a project and a set of instructions. But I didn't make it clear what was really expected. Using rubrics and explicitly explaining the rubric, giving students the opportunity to evaluate others' work on the rubric has helped to increase the quality of work my students produce. I don't rush things as much and have come to learn that the process and the managing of the process is important.*
>
> —CARRIE REEVE, physical education teacher, LMS

CONCLUSION

All administrative teams will have strong beliefs and expectations for professional learning and growth for their school staff. Building a UDL culture through a professional learning community may be one of the most meaningful ways to promote professional growth and collaboration among staff members. Providing planning time and taking risks while implementing the UDL Guidelines will create an environment in which all will feel comfortable, be motivated to learn, and be willing to make informed decisions based on the needs of their students. It can be extremely powerful when a staff knows that their own learning is just as important as that of their students. To administrators and school leaders who have the desire to build a UDL culture through a PLC, my advice is to learn, listen, share, reflect, and enjoy the fascinating journey.

6

Transforming High School Learning Environments: Our UDL Implementation Journey at César E. Chávez High School

Rene Sanchez, Elizabeth Berquist, and Kirsten Omelan

GUIDING QUESTIONS

■ How can Universal Design for Learning (UDL) implementation occur in a large, decentralized urban school district?

■ What does UDL implementation look like in a large high school?

■ How are teachers and leaders supported during the UDL implementation process?

This chapter describes a multiyear Universal Design for Learning project through the lens of one school's UDL leadership team, dubbed Transforming High School Learning Environments (UDL-THSLE). The UDL-THSLE project is a collaboration between César E. Chávez High School in Houston, the Region 4 (Texas) Educational Service Center (ESC), and All In Education, an education consultancy. This chapter will demonstrate how a committed group of leaders and teachers can move UDL from being just "one more thing" to the central framework that drives the vision, instruction, and learning on a high school campus.

INTRODUCTION TO CHÁVEZ HIGH SCHOOL

César E. Chávez High School (hereafter Chávez or the campus), part of the Houston (Texas) Independent School District (HISD), began its UDL journey during the summer of 2014, when Region 4 ESC requested proposals from high schools willing to engage in a multiyear UDL implementation project. Region 4 ESC is one of twenty regional education service centers established by the Texas Legislature in 1967 to help school districts and charter schools improve efficiency and student performance. Regional education service centers are nonregulatory, intermediate education units. School districts have the option to be served by and participate with a regional education service center, which provides services such as professional development and technical assistance. Region 4 partnered with All In Education, a group of Maryland-based educational consultants, to design and implement a multiyear UDL project for high schools. Maryland is the first state in the nation to have legislation about UDL, and Region 4 was eager to partner with a group that had extensive experience in its implementation. Region 4 and All In Education held a conference call to share information about the UDL framework and recruit interested schools.

During the call, Chávez learned that UDL is a framework that provides multiple ways of presenting information to students, assessing their knowledge, and fostering their engagement to ensure that the school curriculum is accessible to all (Kraglund-Gauthier, Young, & Kell, 2014). This framework was of great interest to the staff at Chávez, which at the time was looking for opportunities to improve the school's special education department in preparation for a move to more inclusive practices during the upcoming school year. They believed the UDL Transforming High School Learning Environments (UDL-THSLE) project would be a good match for the school, and so they applied. Shortly thereafter, Chávez was pleased to learn that Region 4 ESC had selected the school as a partner in the project and the staff began their journey toward UDL implementation.

To provide some context: The Chávez High School opened in 2000 to address overcrowding in two other HISD high schools, whose student populations were approaching 4,000. As of 2016, Chávez served 2,300 students from its attendance zone, as well as approximately 900 others from HISD, for a total of 3,200. The HISD population, which included more than 215,000 students in over 283 schools, was composed as follows: 82 percent Hispanic, 25 percent African American, 3 percent Asian (Vietnamese), 1.5 percent White, and 0.5 percent Other; 76 percent of these students qualified for free and reduced-price lunch. The student population of Chávez was 62 percent Hispanic, 13 percent African American, 3.6 percent Asian, 8.3 percent White, and 1.2 percent Other; 82 percent qualify for free and reduced-price lunch. In 2014, HISD's graduation rates for four-year grads was 81.8 percent, and 84.7 percent for five-year grads. Chávez's graduation rate for four-year grads was 82.9 percent, and 8.2 percent for five-year grads. Chávez's English language learner population is 11.6 percent, and the special education rate is 8.3 percent.

UDL—One of Many Initiatives

Chávez High School can be considered HISD's "initiative central" (Table 6.1). During the 2014–2015 school year, Chávez was the location of many of the district's major initiatives aimed at improving instruction. For example, Chávez was in the second year of PowerUp, HISD's 1:1 laptop computer rollout that also required teachers to learn to use the district's new learning management system, Learning. They also were in the first year of Linked Learning, HISD's plan to create smaller learning communities within schools in order to meet the requirements of a newly won Race to the Top grant from the federal government. Linked Learning required that the staff be trained to implement a program called Capturing Kids' Hearts, which was designed to increase student engagement with staff.

Chávez was also in the first year of Leading Exceptional Schools, a plan aimed at improving school culture. Moreover, to comply with HISD's emphasis on advanced academics, Chávez was offering students and teachers extra training and preparation in taking the PSAT, SAT, and Advanced Placement (AP) exams.

During the second year of the UDL-THSLE project, the National Math and Science Institute (NMSI) complemented the UDL work. At that time Chávez also chose to apply to become an International Baccalaureate Diploma School. Finally, due to the large number of newly arrived immigrants at Chávez, HISD labeled it a Newcomer Hub School. This meant Chávez would serve not only its own newcomers but also those from other area schools.

It may not seem important to articulate these connections between initiatives, since all of them were designed to have a positive impact on the students and the schools. However, to the teachers and administrators tasked with leading, teaching, and running a safe and orderly school, the multitude of initiatives began to seem disconnected and became frustrating. In the midst of these myriad initiatives and responsibilities, Chávez embarked on the multiyear UDL-THSLE project.

TABLE 6.1 District and Chávez initiatives by year of implementation

DISTRICTWIDE INITIATIVES		
YEAR 2013–2014	**2014–2015**	**2015–2016**
PowerUp	PowerUp	PowerUp
	The HUB, LMS	The HUB, LMS
	National Math and Science Initiative	National Math and Science Initiative
		Capturing Kids' Hearts
SAT and AP emphasis	PSAT, SAT, and AP emphasis	PSAT, SAT, and AP emphasis
	Leading Exceptional Schools	Leading Exceptional Schools
CHAVEZ SCHOOL INITIATIVES		
YEAR 2013–2014	**2014–2015**	**2015–2016**
	Newcomer Hub	Newcomer Hub
	International Baccalaureate	International Baccalaureate
Inclusion (full)	Inclusion (full)	Inclusion (full)
Universal Design for Learning	Universal Design for Learning	Universal Design for Learning

YEAR ONE: EXPLORATION TO INTEGRATION

The UDL-THSLE project offered multiple professional learning opportunities designed to guide the Chávez staff from UDL exploration to integration. CAST (2012) has described five phases of UDL implementation: (1) exploration, (2) preparation, (3) integration, (4) scaling, and (5) optimizing. Based on the work of Fixsen, Naoom, Blase, Friedman, and Wallace (2005), this model was designed to be a flexible, iterative process.

The collaborative team from Region 4 ESC and All In Education relied on the work of CAST and their own experiences with UDL implementation, as well as lessons learned from implementation efforts by the Baltimore County Public School System and the Bartholomew Consolidated School Corporation (BCSC) in Columbus, Indiana (see *www.udlcenter.org/implementation/fourdistricts*). All schools are unique, and the UDL-THSLE project was not designed to be a lock-step process. When Region 4 ESC and All In Education designed the school's professional learning opportunities, they understood that the Chávez faculty would be at different places at different times throughout the implementation process. Much of the initial work took place in two professional learning communities (PLCs)—the teacher professional learning community (TPLC) and the administrator/leadership professional learning community (LPLC)—each of which had to meet specific requirements, as did members of the entire professional staff.

Exploration

The purpose of the exploration phase is to investigate UDL as a framework for decision making, raise awareness about UDL among decision makers, and determine their interest and willingness to pursue UDL implementation (National Center on Universal Design for Learning, 2012). The UDL exploration phase at Chávez was sparked by a desire to learn more about instructional strategies to meet the needs of diverse learners. The UDL framework, with its flexibility and focus on proactive options, promised a viable way to support effective instruction for all learners, not just those with disabilities.

Preparation

When a school is preparing to implement UDL, the focus is on creating a school climate that accepts variability. School leaders are encouraged to reflect on existing policies that may or may not support UDL, such as organizational and personnel structures. Finally, those leading the process must establish a vision and an implementation action plan (National Center on Universal Design for Learning, 2012). At the start of the school year, the UDL-THSLE leadership team (All In Education, Region 4 ESC, and Chávez administrators) introduced UDL to the staff during a schoolwide professional development session, and the entire faculty was invited to participate in a book study of *Universal Design for Learning: Theory and Practice* (Meyer, Rose, & Gordon, 2014). The purpose of the book study was to build awareness of the UDL framework so that all staff, not just those engaged in the PLCs, would have a foundational understanding of UDL for their future work. Unfortunately, only about 15 percent of faculty participated in the book study and associated learning activities; those who did were paid a stipend out of district funds.

The TPLC and LPLC were formed to support the move from preparation to integration. The TPLC consisted of teachers assigned to the ninth-grade inclusion team, and the LPLC consisted of administrators assigned to evaluate that team. Throughout year one, the TPLC prepared to integrate UDL in their classrooms. During early release professional development days they would review a chapter from Meyer, Rose, and Gordon's book (2014) and consider the content through hands-on activities, and then reflect on practice. After each PLC session, the teachers were expected to apply what they had learned in their classroom; the process was repeated during Saturday professional development sessions. The Chávez LPLC also met on early release days to explore the UDL framework as a basis for decision making. The planning team was careful to distinguish between a PLC meeting and a PD session. PLC meetings were driven by the participants and were focused on group problem solving and movement toward a common goal of instructional transformation using UDL. PD sessions were designed to meet individual learning needs and were led by outside consultants and administrators.

Integration

CAST suggests providing professional learning opportunities to develop educator expertise during the UDL implementation phase (National Center on Universal Design for Learning, 2012). The Chávez leadership team was tasked with creating processes, resources, and protocols to support UDL implementation at the school. Throughout year one, the TPLC and LPLC held monthly meetings to build capacity in applying the UDL framework to instructional and leadership practices. Both PLCs also engaged in Saturday sessions that focused on specific needs they had identified during the monthly meetings. As an added incentive, TPLC and LPLC members who attended the Saturday sessions received a stipend.

The UDL-THSLE leadership team worked to ensure that the PLC meetings focused on discussion and application, and that the professional development sessions provided Chávez staff with new information. Teachers also had the opportunity to engage in 1:1 or small-group lesson-planning sessions. Refining their lesson planning with a UDL expert was a step toward applying knowledge to instruction. The PLC coaches from All In Education and Region 4 ESC collaborated with Chávez administrators and conducted monthly classroom walkthroughs as a way to collect formative data on classroom instruction and the application of UDL, and then shared patterns they found that related to the UDL Guidelines. This information drove PLC conversations, as well as future professional development topics.

Year one also included visits to Baltimore County, Maryland, where a UDL PLC project had been under way for three years. These visits allowed team members to see UDL in practice and discuss the implementation journey with educators and administrators who had participated in a similar process. To support future capacity-building efforts, all content from each TPLC, LPLC, and Saturday session was maintained on a UDL Connect online community site (see Table 6.2 for year-one feedback from the TPLCs and LPLCs). At the end of year one, the project leadership team met to review progress made toward the UDL-THSLE goals and to design a plan for moving toward the integration phase at Chávez. The team also compared formative feedback for fall and spring from faculty who had participated in the TPLC and LPLC.

Year One: Barriers and Solutions

The initial TPLC consisted of the teachers who taught in inclusive classrooms. They were selected, rather than recruited, to participate. This made for a rocky start—there was participation but not necessarily buy-in. This feeling extended to the administration, including the principal, except for two assistant principals who were participating in the LPLC. By the end of the first semester, several TPLC members were struggling with both their classes and the expectations of the UDL-THSLE project. They were working with large ninth-grade classes and were struggling to meet the challenges of learner variability and frustrated with the additional responsibilities of participation in a PLC. They believed their time should be spent discussing students who were having difficulties in their courses, rather than focusing on instruction. They were unable to see the link between strong instructional practice and student engagement (see Table 6.2 for feedback from TPLC and LPLC members).

TABLE 6.2 Year-one TPLC and LPLC feedback, fall and spring

	FALL	SPRING
TPLC PARTICIPANTS	• Felt anxious • Had difficulty seeing connections to the project as a process and not a quick fix • Did not see where UDL fit in appraisal • Needed explicit UDL connections	• Were moving away from asking what teachers are doing to looking at what the students are doing • Had a better feeling for the expectations • Those who "showed up" were very motivated and optimistic
LPLC PARTICIPANTS	• Asked how UDL connects with current initiatives • Asked what their role is in this project	• Felt much more comfortable with the UDL Guidelines and framework • Could talk to those they appraised about how to apply UDL to strengthen instruction

The UDL-THSLE leadership team identified strategies to help these TPLC members buy in to the project. At one point, the leadership team identified options that existed in their classrooms that aligned with the UDL framework, but this backfired, because some members of the TPLC believed they were "already doing UDL" and thus tuned out. They may in fact have been implementing some strategies aligned with the UDL framework, but they were not being thoughtful or proactive and were certainly not considering all learners in the design of their learning environment. Offering choice once during a period is not necessarily enough. Allowing students to "think, pair, share" is not enough. Allowing students to draw or sing their exit ticket is not enough. It is true that UDL implementation begins with the conception of the lesson and a plan to address the variability in all learners, but it is a way of thinking about teaching and learning, not a strategy or a tool. Although academic programs are frequently geared toward the "average" students, the average student does not exist (Tzivinikou, 2014). Without a strong conceptual understanding of UDL, it is impossible to fully integrate the framework into instruction. The UDL-THSLE leadership realized that to help the TPLC make this conceptual shift, they would first need to bring about change with the LPLC.

During the second semester of year one, when the administration began planning for the 2015–2016 school year, the principal had an epiphany, which occurred as they were looking for ways to connect the myriad initiatives that bedeviled teachers. As the school year had progressed, other school and district initiatives and daily responsibilities began to creep into each teacher's purview at the school. The administration had attempted to give All In Education initiatives the same level of importance, but the quality of implementation had begun to suffer.

The principal's epiphany coincided with a tragedy that occurred at Chávez. One spring day, several central office administrators were scheduled to perform walkthroughs and discuss aligning the various initiatives. Just before the school day began, however, school administrators received word that one of their students had passed away the night before. Although Chávez is large, it is a close-knit community, and any event such as a sudden death or a hospitalization affects the entire campus. Despite seeing the need to serve the school community's feelings in a difficult time, the central office administrators still felt it necessary to meet to discuss their initiatives, conduct walkthroughs, and reflect on what they observed. As the hours passed, the principal observed students, teachers, and members of HISD's psychological services move in and out of the library, which had been set up as a makeshift counseling center, and he could not help but wonder how the campus was responding to the loss of the student. When the walkthroughs were over and the visitors and staff met to reflect, the principal was reminded of a verse from a song by They Might Be Giants called "One Everything," in which the singer imagines drawing a giant circle around everything, so nothing or no one would ever be "outside." This moment was a turning point for UDL implementation, and would significantly affect progress during year two at Chávez.

It was while the administration was supporting the campus in its time of grief and planning for the 2015–2016 school year that the principal had his epiphany. He stood up at a meeting that was meant to focus on initiatives but was overshadowed by tragedy, and told the group that teaching and learning are everything in the classroom. He drew an imaginary circle around the school and the classroom, and explained that anything outside the circle that was not a component of teaching and learning should not be allowed to interfere with the process on the inside. He spoke about the importance of affect and engagement in the classroom and, for the first time, shared his understanding that the UDL framework was unique because it put the affective network on the same level as the strategic and recognition networks. While he was considering the affective needs of the school and the importance of community, he decided not to wait for the district to align the initiatives but to form his own plan for operationalizing the myriad initiatives at Chávez.

Katz and Sugden (2013) stressed the importance of campus administrators by including them as the third block in their three-block model. Their role was to manage systemic structures, such as handling funding and assigning planning time and professional development, so UDL could be implemented. At Chávez, the LPLC realized that they needed to give the staff a clear understanding of how UDL fit in with other school priorities and explain specifically how UDL was part of the school structure.

In early spring, the LPLC met with the UDL-THSLE leadership team and a consultant from a partner district to plan protocols that would help them align their initiatives. The LPLC began by listing all major initiatives on the campus and then identifying the "look-fors" that corresponded to each initiative. This information was distilled into six categories that are essential in each classroom: (1) student choice and flexibility, (2) environment and culture, (3) rigor, (4) effective lesson design and delivery, (5) student engagement, and (6) data-driven decisions. Finally, the team aligned each initiative with a related category or categories. They presented this in a graphic titled "Chávez: Instruction and Relationships in Classrooms and Learning Environments," or the Chávez Circle, that represented Chávez's personalized framework for UDL, dubbed Effective First Teach.

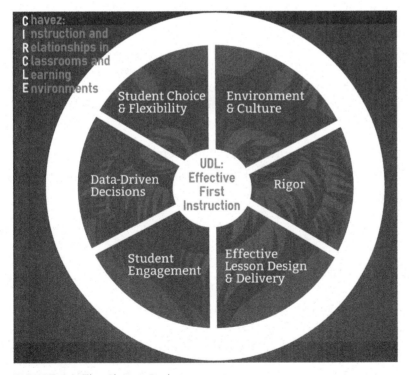

FIGURE 6.1 The Chávez Circle

To help promote greater understanding, the LPLC aligned the six categories to HISD's Teacher Appraisal and Development System (TADS). The LPLC was hopeful that this representation would guide future work and remove the barrier that people still viewed UDL as just "one more thing" (see Figure 6.1 for representations of the Chávez Circle).

An additional barrier in year one was that both the TPLC and LPLC said they "did not know what UDL looked like" in action. Fortunately, the UDL-THSLE leadership team was able to connect the PLC members with staff at Lansdowne Middle School (chapter 5) and Halstead Academy (see chapter 4) in Baltimore County, Maryland, where UDL implementation was well under way. Chávez sent three groups to observe at these schools. The Houston school calendar ended earlier than Baltimore County; therefore, the Chávez principal and lead UDL assistant principal could see classes in session, meet with students, participate in PLC planning sessions, and speak with leaders at Lansdowne and Halstead. The principal said the visit was a turning point for him, both personally and professionally:

> Since the Baltimore County visit, my life and career as an instructional leader have taken on a new and different meaning. All of my conversations and observations now utilize a design thinking mindset. All students can learn and show that they understand if given the methods through which they can be successful and engaged. All teachers can grow to become the instructors and guides that their students need.

He added that the Baltimore visit gave him a new appreciation for "the dexterity" UDL provides to both teachers and learners. As a result of this new understanding, Effective First Teach would become the mantra for preparing for year two.

YEAR TWO: INTEGRATION AND SCALING

Goals for year two included continued integration and scaling. The UDL-THSLE leadership team recognized that Chávez staff members would be at different places at different times in the UDL implementation process and thus thoughtfully designed professional learning opportunities that were appropriate for those new to UDL and for those who had participated in the book study or TPLC. Strategies for integration in year two included:

- Reestablishing returning TPLC and LPLC members' commitment

- Recruiting new TPLC members through an application process

- Holding a two-day UDL institute for the entire campus administrative team

- Holding a three-day co-teaching institute for co-teach partnerships

- Holding half-day campus-wide UDL professional development and break-out sessions at the beginning of the school year

- Sharing UDL as the guiding curricular framework with community partners at the annual Chávez Partnership Breakfast

- Holding a campus-wide book study on *UDL Now!* (Novak, 2014)

- Holding early dismissal professional development sessions on UDL for non-cohort teachers and leaders

- Continuing TPLC and LPLC in-depth study and application of UDL

- Continuing the professional development "Saturday sessions" with stipends

- Observing classes at BCSC in Columbus, Indiana

- Using "UDL Spotlight" to integrate the UDL language into the instructional feedback process for all teachers

- Aligning the district TADS to the UDL Guidelines

- Teaching administrators and teachers outside the PLCs to conduct ghost walks (walks occurring without teachers or students present) and provide quality feedback

- Engaging the campus in social emotional professional development aimed at developing strategies for multiple means of engagement

- Conducting UDL instructional rounds

Scaling UDL involves enhancing effective processes and organizational supports and expanding UDL practices throughout the school or community. As a result of thoughtful preparation and the integration of UDL into the leadership team vision, the project leadership team launched the Chávez Circle, which had been developed at the end of year one. The Chávez Circle provided a constant visual representation of the campus initiatives' alignment with UDL as the guiding curricular and instructional framework for Effective First Teach. The Chávez Circle was first launched at a two-day summer training for the Chávez administrative team, the Linked Learning Pathway Team leads, the content-area team leads, the department chairs, and guests from the HISD. The UDL-THSLE leadership team brought the group together at the University of Houston to ensure that all school leaders received the same focused message about UDL. The Chávez administrative team was adamant that these leaders be surrounded by the language, the visuals, and the expectations of UDL and Effective First Teach.

Before the start of the school year, the Chávez administration hosted two weeks of professional development designed around the Chávez Circle. The entire school was also trained in Capturing Kids' Hearts, a behavioral improvement program that aims to increase student engagement by building rapport with and among learners. During "Circle sessions," all staff members received an outline of the six categories, which they explored with interactive, applicable professional learning activities. After each session, participants received a sticker representing the piece of the Chávez Circle they had explored. The center of the circle read "UDL: Effective First Teach." This was an additional strategy for surrounding Chávez staff with the expectations of UDL and Effective First Teach.

The entire staff was also given a copy of *UDL Now! A Teacher's Monday Morning Guide to Implementing the Common Core State Standards Using Universal Design for Learning*, by Katie Novak (2014). *UDL Now!* offers teachers an engaging way to learn more about UDL while providing them with strategies to use immediately. Texas has its own standards, but teachers understood they were to replace references to Common Core with references to Texas Essential Knowledge and Skills.

Another process that needed to reflect the UDL framework was our common board configuration. The traditional common board displays the state standard: the outline for the day's lesson, homework assignments, and any upcoming tests or quizzes. The TPLC and LPLC recommended that this information be summarized in three essential questions that aligned with the UDL framework. They wanted to ensure that a student, an appraiser, a superintendent, or a visitor from another school district would be able to determine a classroom's goals for the day. The three questions the PLCs developed were:

What am I learning?

Why am I learning it?

How will I know I have learned it?

Participants agreed that the first question, "What am I learning?," should be a rewriting of the state content or process standard or the specific part of the standard to be addressed that day during class. It should not be a single word or phrase, nor should it refer to an activity scheduled for that class day.

They agreed that the second question, "Why am I learning it?," is the teacher's opportunity to engage the student in learning by showing relevance or a future purpose. Teachers should show students how what is being taught that day is applicable to the real world, or how they might use it later in the year in that class or in a future class in the same content area. Engagement is one of the most important tenets of UDL—increasing student interest and motivation provides an opportunity for deeper learning (Lopes-Murphy, 2012; Tzivinikou, 2014).

The third question, "How will I know I have learned it?," would empower the students to articulate their ability to mastery content. Teachers agreed that this question should be written as a specific metric or event that will allow students to know that they have mastered the objective, and not as "mastery on the test" or "when you complete the worksheet." Ideally, what is written on the common board will give the students a clear explanation of what is expected of them that day in class. At Chávez, these expectations were aligned with the UDL framework and became the norm in each classroom.

Year Two: UDL Professional Learning

All professional learning options in year two were directly connected to the Chávez Circle. During each early release professional development day, school leaders offered sessions that helped all staff members enhance their knowledge of choice and flexibility, environment and culture, rigor, effective lesson design and delivery, student engagement, and data-driven decisions. After each session, staff were asked to reflect using a Google Doc, and their reflections were used to plan the next professional learning session. Most importantly, teachers were asked to propose ideas for new learning and to share their own skills with colleagues by conducting or participating in future sessions. Setting clear goals for professional learning, encouraging reflection and revision, and fostering community and collaboration among the staff during early release days modeled the UDL framework in practice. Chávez leaders expected staff to apply UDL in their classroom practice, but they were holding themselves to the same standards.

The year-two TPLC teachers also participated in the professional learning sessions, but they always worked together as a PLC, and all PLC meeting agendas were determined by the members of the TPLC. In year two, every TPLC member decided to participate in the UDL-THSLE project, which led to a great deal of buy-in and enthusiasm for integrating UDL into their practice. The TPLC members were focused on their individual success, but they were also concerned with the success of the group. During PLC sessions, they applied content from monthly readings of *UDL Now!* to their own classrooms, shared ideas and strategies for removing learning barriers, and, most importantly, celebrated each other's work and built each other up when things were not going as planned. In year two, the TPLC finally became a true learning community.

This group was incredibly dedicated to their own professional learning. Because the professional development sessions held on early release days were focused on building their PLC, the TPLC teachers needed to find time to focus on professional development. They enthusiastically agreed to attend

Saturday sessions throughout the year. The LPLC also attended Saturday sessions, which ensured that all PLC members were receiving the same information. At each Saturday session, the group focused on a UDL Guideline, appropriate strategies for putting the Guideline into practice, and created a tool or resource they could implement immediately (this was known as a "Make for Monday").

The year-two professional learning options included a visit to the Bartholomew Consolidated School Corporation (BCSC) in Indiana, an early adopter of UDL (see chapter 8 for Bartholomew's story). This experience significantly influenced several of the more experienced educators in the TPLC and LPLC, because it allowed them to see how UDL can flourish in both comprehensive high schools and in elementary, middle, and magnet schools. One of the key takeaways from the visit was the emphasis on the design of proactive learning environments and the thoughtful use of space. Both the TPLC and LPLC members were inspired by the visit and motivated to identify more proactive, flexible supports for all learners.

In BCSC, UDL is half of the teacher-evaluation rubric, and the visit prompted the LPLC to reevaluate their role in providing feedback to teachers. Although UDL is not included in the TADS, the Chávez administration recognized the importance of providing specific, mastery-oriented feedback related to the UDL implementation. Teachers were encouraged to use formative feedback in the classroom in order to make instructional decisions, and the LPLC members knew they needed to model this strategy. They also were inspired by a visit to an HISD feeder elementary school to consider giving formative feedback, and one PLC meeting focused on increasing the number of conversations about UDL held in the school. The Chávez principal tasked the LPLC with creating a tool to share quick, effective feedback, and the group decided that the feedback form should be aligned with the Chávez Circle.

To facilitate fast but focused feedback, the LPLC created a series of sentence starters that aligned with the UDL framework. This focused feedback, provided by the leadership team to teachers, focused on multiple means of representation, engagement, action, and expression. In this way, all coaches, appraisers, and visitors could use UDL language to provide feedback. The LPLC also decided to use a carbon form that could be quickly split into sheets, so the teacher would receive immediate feedback and the person who completed the form could maintain a record of their feedback. Using this feedback tool was critical as the Chávez leadership began to expand the Effective First Teach beyond the TPLC and LPLC. In ensuring that all staff was receiving feedback aligned with the UDL framework, they were already beginning to move from integrating to scaling. This gave the LPLC the opportunity to analyze feedback to determine where they needed to improve how they articulated specific feedback aligned with the UDL framework.

Year-two professional learning culminated with UDL rounds, a two-day structured protocol designed to give PLC members insight into their practice. All PLC members had the opportunity to teach, to be observed, and to make the rounds and observe their colleagues. The UDL-THSLE leadership team invited current TPLC and LPLC members to participate, along with other educators in the district who were interested in learning more about UDL implementation.

The UDL rounds process was facilitated by UDL experts who led the group in identifying a problem of practice on day one. The group set norms and goals and clearly articulated expectations for the rounds. It is important to note that the process was based on coaching and growth, not on evaluation. The rounds occurred over two days, and each day ended with a structured debriefing that focused on observations and analysis relative to the UDL framework. On day two, the final activity challenged the PLC to summarize their observations of current practice in order to identify personal and group goals for year three. TPLC and LPLC members reflected on this process, identifying UDL rounds as a powerful tool for facilitating collaboration, developing a common language, refining their own practices, and setting goals for future UDL implementation. Table 6.3 presents selected individual and group goals developed by the TPLC and LPLC members.

TABLE 6.3 Year-three goals

INDIVIDUAL GOALS	GROUP GOALS
Help students sustain effort and persistence so that all are challenged regardless of where they start	Create a repository of shared resources that support application of the UDL framework
Learn to facilitate student-led activities and student-led conferences	Identify additional opportunities to see UDL in practice: at Chávez, in neighboring HISD schools, and in other districts and states
Develop strategies to engage students in the learning process through small-group activities and stations	Focus on UDL in assessment; plan professional learning sessions that focus on both formative and summative assessment options

MOVING FORWARD

As the UDL-THSLE leadership team prepared to begin the third year of implementation in 2016–2017, they planned to expand the project to include an additional PLC; they were enthusiastic about the potential to scale this work to more than 180 teachers. They were also dedicated to finding ways to incorporate the most important stakeholders in the UDL implementation process: the students. The team wanted to develop students' capacity to serve as UDL experts and evaluators, and envisioned students coaching students on how to develop choice within the context of their own learning. In year three, the UDL-THSLE leadership team also will design supportive ways for Region 4 ESC and All In Education to transfer more of the PLC and professional learning leadership responsibilities to the campus leadership team. Strategies for integration and scaling in year three include:

- Continued recruitment of staff members for a second TPLC through an interest meeting and application process

- Inclusion of current PLC members in the recruitment process

- Celebrations of learning and classroom application among the current TPLC members

- Testimonials by current TPLC members to the campus regarding UDL implementation in their classrooms

- Investigation of how the campus leadership team might take the lead in supporting the current TPLC

- Exploration of and preparation for student involvement in campus-wide UDL implementation efforts

- Continued support for current LPLC and TPLC dates for the year (one per month)

- Continued professional "Saturday sessions" learning opportunities

- Continued visits to other UDL implementation sites

- A one- or two-day UDL institute for new staff, or for returning staff who would like to extend their learning with the current PLC members leading and designing the institute

- UDL instructional rounds

- End-of-year campus celebration

- Creative incentives for participation

- Research on how to structure campus schedules and assignment of responsibilities in order to designate certain staff members as UDL facilitators

Ironically, several of the initiatives related to the Chávez Circle were cycling down and will no longer be expectations of the district. Nevertheless, the UDL-THSLE leadership team was confident that the Chávez Circle will easily weather any changes because its foundation is Universal Design for Learning. In using UDL as the foundation, Chávez leadership was able to clearly articulate areas of focus that are applicable in all learning environments. This is the power of the UDL framework. No matter what the initiative is, the framework provides a lens through which educators can consider their learning environments. It is an instructional framework for design, delivery, self-assessment, and continuous improvement. The Chávez Circle also serves as a filter that helps the campus leadership determine if something will be instructionally productive for the school. If it does not align with the Chávez Circle, it will not happen at Chávez. The UDL framework will continue to guide Chávez in its efforts to create a successful learning environment for every learner.

7

A Co-Teaching Conversation: Using UDL to Co-Plan for the Inclusive Classroom

Kavita Rao and Elizabeth Berquist

GUIDING QUESTIONS

- How can general and special education teachers use Universal Design for Learning (UDL) when they co-teach?

- How can UDL and co-teaching approaches be considered during the lesson-planning process?

- How can co-teachers use UDL to ensure that students with and without disabilities can engage meaningfully and learn core knowledge and skills in standards-based lessons?

This chapter illustrates how general and special education co-teaching teams can use UDL in their classrooms to design inclusive instructional environments and lessons that support students with and without disabilities. We describe how co-teachers can apply UDL to goals, assessments, methods, and materials, and provide an example of a "co-teaching conversation" that illustrates how a general education and special education teacher can incorporate UDL into a standards-based lesson.

INTRODUCTION: LAYING THE GROUNDWORK

Ms. Reese and Ms. Kim are co-teachers in an inclusive eighth-grade classroom. In the year they have worked together, they have tried using several of the co-teaching models they learned about in a series of in-service trainings offered by their school. Currently, the general education teacher Ms. Reese develops the lesson plan and emails it to Ms. Kim, the special education teacher. Ms. Kim then modifies it to address the needs of the students in the class who have disabilities. The teachers usually chat briefly before class and then launch into their roles—teaching and supporting students. For the upcoming school year, Ms. Reese and Ms. Kim want to use strategies they learned in a professional development workshop about collaboratively planning and integrating strategies that can support all learners, those with and without disabilities. They decide to use a portion of their prep time to develop lessons together using the UDL framework and to have collaborative planning conversations.

Many schools use inclusion models to ensure that students with disabilities can be placed in the least restrictive and inclusive environments appropriate for their needs. Co-teaching plays a key part in an inclusion model by providing a structure for general and special educators to pool their skills and expertise to create lessons that support all learners. Co-teaching leverages the expertise that both teachers bring to the classroom. Thus, an essential element of co-teaching is parity; the general and special education teachers are equals who share their expertise and bring together their knowledge about content and instructional strategies to plan lessons that address the needs of all learners.

Murawski and Lochner (2010) describe how co-teachers can work together during the instructional planning and implementation process. To ensure that both teachers take responsibility for planning and implementing instruction, they suggest co-planning, co-instructing, and co-assessing. The special education teacher, for example, can provide expertise on differentiated strategies, accommodations, and modifications for students receiving special education services. However, the planning lessons they create together should include scaffolds and supports for all students.

Friend and Cook (2012) describe six approaches to co-teaching: (1) teaming, (2) parallel teaching, (3) station teaching, (4) one teaching, one assisting, (5) alternative teaching, and (6) one teaching, one observing (see the sidebar "Six Co-Teaching Approaches"). Co-teachers can use these approaches, as appropriate, while implementing lessons, and may use more than one. For example, they may start a lesson by teaming and then moving to station teaching to work with small groups. They can choose which approaches to use during the co-planning process and select those that support the instructional activities they have planned.

Six Co-Teaching Approaches

Here are the six co-teaching approaches described by Friend and Cook (2012):

- Teaming—Both teachers deliver instruction to all students.

- Parallel teaching—Teachers divide the class and teach the same information.

- Station teaching—Teachers divide the content and students circulate among stations to work with each teacher on specific areas.

- One teach, one assist—One teacher takes primary responsibility for teaching, while the other circulates to assist students as needed.

- Alternative teaching—One teacher works with a large group, while the other focuses on a small group.

- One teach, one observe—One teacher observes students and collects data during instruction, and both teachers discuss and analyze the data.

For more information, see the Co-Teaching Connection website: *www.marilynfriend.com.*

Some foundational precursors and contextual factors must be in place to give co-teachers the knowledge and skills to co-plan, co-instruct, and co-assess. Administrators play a key role in setting the stage for schoolwide adoption of co-teaching. To create a foundation for successful collaboration between general and special education teachers, all teachers should be offered professional development on what co-teaching is, what the co-teaching approaches are, and how to plan and teach collaboratively. The professional development also should give teachers insights into how to establish co-teaching relationships and enable them to practice the collaboration and communication skills needed to co-plan, co-instruct, and co-assess.

Administrators can also support the logistical needs of co-teaching teams by ensuring that they have sufficient time to work together by providing planning periods in which they prepare their lessons collaboratively. Ideally, special education teachers will be assigned to no more than two general education teachers—they cannot establish successful co-teaching relationships if their time is divided among too many. This also can ensure that the special education teacher does not get relegated to the role of an assistant who only helps carry out a lesson plan already designed by the general education teacher.

CO-TEACHING WITH A UDL LENS

A typical inclusion classroom is made up of general education students and those receiving special education services, students who have Section 504 accommodations, and those who are culturally and linguistically diverse. Focusing on instruction for the students receiving special education services often is seen as the domain of the special education teacher, including ensuring that students with disabilities receive the necessary modifications and accommodations.

Although some students are identified as needing services, learner variability is not limited to these students. The reality is that all learners have varying abilities, backgrounds, interests, and challenges, and everyone can benefit when lessons are designed to support a range of learners. UDL provides a structure for designing lessons that include flexible options that can benefit all learners. By considering UDL Guidelines while co-planning, teachers can integrate flexible supports and scaffolds from the outset, thus reducing the need to make individual modifications. However, it is important to note that some students may still need specific modifications and accommodations to address their IEP objectives. For example, the special education teacher will need to ensure that students who have a visual impairment or a specific behavioral strategy on their IEP receive the specific tools or strategies they need.

UDL has three main principles—providing multiple means of representation, multiple means of action and expression, and multiple means of engagement (Meyer, Rose, & Gordon, 2014)—as well as nine Guidelines and thirty-one checkpoints that define how to apply the three principles to instruction.

> *See the website of the National Center on Universal Design for Learning (2014;* www.udlcenter.org/aboutudl/udlguidelines) *for an interactive graphic that provides detailed information on the UDL Guidelines and checkpoints, including examples of how they can be applied to lessons.*

UDL provides an organizational framework for integrating flexible and differentiated practices into a lesson. The UDL Guidelines offer a menu of options from which teachers can choose to design lessons that are flexible, provide choices and options, and engage students (Hall, Meyer, & Rose, 2012; Meyer et al., 2014). The guidelines also give general and special educators a shared language they can use to discuss their lesson goals and plan the assessments, methods, and materials to teach the skills and content within the lesson. Teachers can select the checkpoints they find most relevant.

Co-teaching with the UDL approach includes considering (1) barriers in the lesson, (2) clear goals for the lesson that are inclusive for all students, (3) how assessments, methods, and materials can be designed to provide supports and scaffolds for all, and (4) how to meet IEP goals for specific students. In this chapter, we provide examples of how co-teachers can use a UDL approach while co-planning a lesson.

A New View of the Learning Environment

When co-planning using a UDL lens, the first consideration is the design of the learning environment of the shared classroom, which co-teachers can discuss prior to planning lessons. This is ideally done at the start of the school year or the co-teaching relationship, thus allowing teachers to discuss ideas and set shared expectations for themselves and their learners.

The learning environment includes the physical layout of the classroom as well as the culture and expectations. Co-teachers can discuss how to set up a classroom so they can use various co-teaching approaches during lessons. In traditional settings, students sit side-by-side in rows of desks and are taught by one teacher at the front of the classroom. In the co-taught classroom, teachers can leverage the fact that there are two people to guide instruction and arrange the classroom spaces to support the co-teaching approaches they will use.

In this section we use the example of Ms. Reese and Ms. Kim's co-teaching collaboration to show how co-teachers can design their learning environment through a UDL lens.

Early in the school year, Ms. Reese and Ms. Kim decide to create various sections in their classroom. They move a set of desks together to encourage collaboration, place a small number of desks in rows for those receiving direct instruction, and move a medium-sized conference table to the side of the room and place chairs around it for small-group work sessions. They also place beanbag chairs and carpet squares in a corner of the room for those seeking a quiet space. They set the three classroom laptops against one wall to give students independent workstations. By designing the classroom this way, the front and back of the room become indistinguishable. The flexible layout addresses the UDL guidelines by providing options for physical action and optimizing individual choice, which lays the foundations for using a variety of co-teaching methods.

Ms. Reese and Ms. Kim also share their ideas about classroom culture and expectations. After discussing their individual expectations, they agree on what they will present to and talk about with the students. They agree that it is important to start the year with a whole-class discussion in which they share their expectations and allow students to give their input, and thus to create a classroom culture that the teachers and students have agreed on together.

They set up structures to encourage students to interact with both teachers. For example, they place colored bins on one wall, where students put their completed work. They put a notebook beside the bins that contains the teachers' schedules, which enables students to sign up for additional help with either teacher, and to select a date and time. On another wall, they place a basket of sticky notes, pens, and a laminated "Ask Me" poster. The directions posted beside the basket state, "If you have a question for Ms. Reese or Ms. Kim, write it down and place it on the poster." Each day, the teachers take turns answering students' questions. Ms. Reese and Ms. Kim also develop phrases to use when giving students feedback so they can use similar language. They hang these phrases on the classroom bulletin board so students see that the teachers have a system for providing consistent feedback. These strategies for establishing a classroom culture are consistent with the UDL checkpoints of providing multiple options for communication, facilitating management of information and resources, providing options for sustaining persistence and effort, and providing mastery-oriented feedback.

CO-PLANNING LESSONS WITH UDL

After making some key decisions on how to structure the learning environment, co-teachers have the ongoing daily task of designing and delivering lessons together. Using UDL to guide their co-planning sessions, teachers can design lessons that build in flexibility and scaffolds. The four-step UDL design cycle addresses four key lesson components—goals, assessments, methods, and materials—and teachers can refer to the UDL Guidelines to consider where and how to provide flexible options for each lesson component (Ralabate, 2016). Throughout this process, teachers can also decide how to co-instruct and which of the six co-teaching approaches to use in their classroom.

Table 7.1 illustrates the four-step process and highlights the questions co-teachers can discuss as they develop inclusive and accessible lessons. By considering the UDL Guidelines, teachers can build in flexible options, scaffolds, and supports for all learners, including students with and without disabilities.

TABLE 7.1 The UDL design cycle

STEPS	QUESTIONS FOR DISCUSSION	CONSIDERING UDL
1. State clear goals	What standards does this lesson address? What are the lesson objectives? What are the barriers in our goals/objectives?	State clear goals for the lesson plan in relation to the standards and overall objectives.
2. Use flexible assessments	How can we use formative assessments that allow students to demonstrate knowledge in various ways? How can we incorporate scaffolds that help students learn the content or skills for the summative assessments? How can we design assessments that reduce barriers to demonstrating knowledge/skills?	Integrate formative assessments that give students varied ways to express what they know. Ensure that the format of expression is not a barrier. When summative assessments are required to be in one format (e.g., a written assessment), provide opportunities for students to practice in that format; when possible, include scaffolds as they practice, strategies they can use when they take the summative assessment.

STEPS	QUESTIONS FOR DISCUSSION	CONSIDERING UDL
3. Design flexible methods	How and when can we provide flexible options during instruction that all learners can benefit from? What options should we include to ensure that students with IEPs have the necessary modifications and accommodations? Should we provide any of these options to all students? Which co-teaching approaches should we use as we co-instruct this lesson? Which approach best supports the teaching and learning activities for this lesson?	Use the UDL Guidelines as a menu and pick a few relevant checkpoints you can address in this lesson. The UDL checkpoints delineate various scaffolds that can be included during instruction and highlight strategies that help students learn key content. Decide how you will co-instruct based on the activities you will include in this lesson. From the six co-teaching approaches (Friend & Cook, 2012), pick one or two to use, depending on the teaching and learning activities for that lesson.
4. Select flexible materials	Are there barriers for any students in the materials we are using? What materials and media can we incorporate to give students options?	Consider what materials, resources and tools can be integrated into the lesson to support and engage students. This can include low- and high-tech options (e.g., manipulatives, technology tools).

An important part of planning with UDL is to identify existing barriers to learning, such as the formats of instructional delivery and assessment. For example, expecting students to demonstrate what they know in writing or to read a text to learn content can pose barriers for some students. Other barriers include students not having the background information required to learn new concepts or students being disengaged in class, which can occur for various reasons. Teachers can refer to the UDL Guidelines and checkpoints to reflect on what and how they are currently teaching and to consider where the barriers may lie for their students. This enables them to design instructional activities from the start that address the barriers by providing flexibility, choice, and options for engagement, instead of modifying a lesson after the fact.

In the next section, we present an example of a co-planning conversation between two teachers, which highlights just one among the many ways to approach lesson planning using a UDL lens.

A Co-Planning Conversation: The *Fault in Our Stars* Lesson

Earlier, we learned how Ms. Reese and Ms. Kim collaborated to set up their learning environment. They work together daily to co-plan, co-instruct, and co-assess, guided by the shared goal of ensuring that all students in their classrooms are being held to high standards and receiving the supports they need. Ms. Reese and Ms. Kim also strive to engage their students by making lessons relevant and giving students choices as they learn.

Ms. Reese and Ms. Kim are designing a series of lessons that address English language arts standards that relate to analyzing a story. Earlier in the month their students read the book *The Fault in Our Stars* (Green, 2012) and watched the movie based on the book in class. Ms. Reese and Ms. Kim decide to plan a series of lessons in which students compare and contrast the book and the movie. This example of a co-planning conversation illustrates how Ms. Reese and Ms. Kim plan the unit using the four-step UDL design cycle and integrate various co-teaching approaches in an eighth-grade classroom.

Step One: State Clear Goals

Ms. Reese: The standard we are addressing for this unit is, "Analyze the extent to which a filmed or live production of a story or drama stays faithful to or departs from the text or script, evaluating the choices made by the director or actors." This standard has several parts. Should we pick a few key skills to address within this standard and develop some clear goal statements?

Ms. Kim: Let's create some "I can" goal statements that address key skills. One thing that jumps out with this standard is the word *analyze*. Let's decide what level of analysis we expect from students and then guide them to compare and contrast the movie and book accordingly.

Ms. Reese: We can include two types of analysis in these lessons: (a) reflection on how the film stays true to or diverges from the book, and (b) making inferences about why the director made choices to stay true to or diverge from the book. Our first goal statement could be, "I can compare and contrast the movie and text versions of *The Fault in Our Stars.*" Our second goal statement could be, "I can describe my opinions on why the director made choices to adapt the book version of *The Fault in Our Stars.*"

Ms. Kim: Okay, let's think about how we can assess these two goals. Then we can come up with our instructional activities in relation to the formative and summative assessments we will use as we teach.

Step Two: Develop Flexible Assessments

Ms. Reese: We also have two "I can" goal statements, so we should design an assessment for each one.

Ms. Kim: For the first goal, we can assess students' ability to compare and contrast by giving them some options to express what they know. The usual assessment method is to let students write a brief constructed response describing similarities and differences. We can add the option of using a visual map to compare and contrast. How about giving students these options: (a) write a constructed response, (b) create a visual map on paper, or (c) create a visual map using the digital graphic organizer on the computer? I know some students love using the online graphic organizer software, and they can access that on the computers in the back of the classroom.

Ms. Reese: I like the idea of providing these three options to all the students. I know some will choose to just write a constructed response, but several will enjoy showing us what they know on a map. And for the two students who have graphic organizers on their IEPs, this ensures that they receive the needed accommodation while a choice for all students.

Ms. Kim: Later we can ask students to use their maps to generate sentences for a constructed response. So, the map option not only serves as a formative assessment for this lesson, it can also become a scaffold for helping students generate a constructed text for an assignment later.

Ms. Reese: For our second assessment, we need to evaluate whether students are able to state their opinions about why the director made certain choices. Should we incorporate some oral presentation skills for this assessment? We can ask students to select one area where the director made a change and present their opinions of why.

Ms. Kim: I like that idea, but I think that might pose barriers for some students. If the assessment is in an oral presentation format, the students who are less comfortable with public speaking may be at a disadvantage. That can also be intimidating to our two English language learners, who feel shy when they are put on the spot to speak. Since the goal of this lesson is not about public speaking, let's make the oral presentation one option. They could do a short oral presentation, create a poster on which they draw a scene and write down why it was different, or work in pairs to do a mock interview where the "director" explains to the "interviewer" why he or she adapted the movie.

Ms. Reese: How are we going to grade these three different formats? I want to be sure that we are assessing the students fairly no matter which format they choose.

Ms. Kim: Let's create a checklist that defines the core information that needs to be there in all three formats. Our core criteria could be something like this: your presentation includes (a) information about one scene from the movie that is not similar to the book, (b) an explanation of how the director modified this scene, and (c) your opinion of why the director changed this scene. We can encourage students to state which version they liked better to let them make a personal connection and have a context for this sort of analysis.

Ms. Reese: Great, I think we have included some good options to assess whether the students are mastering the goals. Now, let's figure out the activities for the lessons within this unit. I think it will take about five class periods to develop this concept, so let's consider how to structure instruction during that time.

Step Three: Design Flexible Methods

Ms. Reese: I'd like to make this whole unit more relevant for them by getting them interested in the idea of comparing movies and books. What's a real-life connection we can make in the first class session when we introduce this lesson?

Ms. Kim: Why don't you ask me a question about a movie I have watched and I can share an example of a time that I read a book and then was disappointed after watching the movie version? I can explain the choices the director made, why I was disappointed by the changes, and why I preferred the book.

Ms. Reese: Great idea. I think hearing you describe how you felt about a movie adapted from a book will be a great hook to draw them into this concept of comparing movies and books.

Ms. Kim: After you give an example, let's have students throw out their opinions on what they liked about the book and the movie as a warm-up. We'll ask them to quietly write down some ideas on their dry-erase boards and then ask volunteers to share ideas. This way, everyone gets the chance to think first, and then those who want to share can speak up.

Ms. Reese: For this warm-up activity, we can use the one teach, one assist approach. I will explain what we want them to do and you can circulate around the room to provide assistance and feedback as they write on their dry-erase boards.

Ms. Kim: After this warm-up, we can start working toward our first goal of comparing and contrasting. Let's use a team teaching approach to model this skill. I will read a short passage from the book and show the corresponding scene from the movie. We will ask students to describe how the scene was similar and different in the two formats. You can lead the discussion, and I will create a map on the whiteboard, using different colors to write up the similarities and differences. This will provide a model for what a map of this information looks like.

Ms. Reese: Good. This approach will help those students who need a refresher on what compare/contrast is and will provide clear guidance on our expectations for all students. This will also serve as formative assessment for us, to see if we need to reteach any areas related to comparing and contrasting. If students seem ready to compare and contrast on their own after we do one example together, we can read another passage together and show the corresponding scene from the movie. Then we can let them try the activity on their own using the three assessment options we discussed before (constructed response, graphic organizer, or digital graphic organizers). If we find that they can use more guidance after we do the first example together, I think we should be prepared to do a second example together as a class.

Ms. Kim: Sounds like a plan.

Ms. Reese: As they do the independent practice, we can both circulate around the room to check in on all students. I'd like to be sure we check in on the students who struggle with these concepts and give them feedback as they work so that they can be successful with the activity too.

Ms. Kim: Okay, we can split up the room. I will check on the students who are making digital graphic organizers and on the students in the tables nearest the computers if you will work with the other side of the room. Let's plan to do these activities over two periods. To end this part of the lesson, we will ask students to turn in their work by putting it in the colored boxes in the back or emailing their work to us if they used the digital graphic organizer. We should remind students to sign up for a meeting with either of us if they have more questions or to post a question on the Ask Me board.

Ms. Reese: After we are done with the first goal, the lessons for the next three class periods can be focused on the second goal: providing their opinions about why the director made certain decisions in the movie. I think this is a more challenging skill. To develop these skills, should we use a parallel teaching approach where we split the class in half and work with two groups separately? That may make it easier to manage a discussion and ensure that all students understand what we expect in regard to "providing an opinion."

Ms. Kim: Good idea. In the small-group format, we can each discuss our own opinions about one scene from the movie and ask students to give their opinions. Once they practice this skill, they can each select another scene and work on formulating an opinion. We can each explain that they will present this opinion in one of three ways we discussed earlier (a short oral presentation, a poster, or a mock interview).

Ms. Reese: Sounds good. For the fourth lesson, we can use a station teaching approach so they can develop their independent work. Let's have a "create," "practice," and "self-reflect" station. At the create station, they can work on their presentations. At the practice station, they can practice their presentation and get feedback from the teacher. At the self-reflect station, we can have copies of the checklist available so that students can evaluate whether their presentations met all criteria. You and I can be at the first two stations and the students can self-evaluate independently at the checklist station.

Step Four: Select Materials and Media

Ms. Reese: What materials and media do we need to gather to ensure that this lesson runs smoothly?

Ms. Kim: We need to select the book passages and related video excerpts from the movie that we'll use for the compare/contrast activities. We should pick at least three so that we have a couple to use for guided practice, if needed, and one for independent activity. We should also print out some paper graphic organizers and put a shortcut to the digital ones on the computers. We need to have a signup sheet and timer for the computer use if a lot of students choose the digital option.

Ms. Reese: Let's use the captioned version of the movie when we show excerpts. That will ensure that our student with a hearing impairment has full access and it will actually benefit the whole class to give them an option to read the text that goes along with the movie.

Ms. Kim: Okay, I will pull out excerpts from the captioned version. Could you prepare the computers with the shortcuts to the digital graphic organizer and print out paper copies as well?

Ms. Reese: Yes, I will. It is so helpful to have two of us to think through this lesson and to organize the materials.

CONCLUSION

The co-teaching conversation between Ms. Reese and Ms. Kim highlights some of the major areas of planning that can be approached together by a co-teaching team. Table 7.2 illustrates which UDL guidelines are addressed by their choices and denotes the co-teaching approaches they use. Like all collaborations, co-teaching conversations will be shaped by the personalities and working styles of the teachers involved. The UDL Guidelines can provide a shared structure and approach for planning together to ensure that both teachers are considering ways to design and deliver flexible and engaging lessons for all the students in their inclusive classrooms.

TABLE 7.2 Co-Teaching conversation: Connections to UDL Guidelines

INSTRUCTIONAL DECISIONS	CONNECTIONS TO UDL GUIDELINES
State clear goals: Teachers created clear "I can" goal statements based on the standard.	Identifying clear goals is a key premise of UDL-based design. Having a clear goal allows teachers to focus on creating activities and assessments that address the goal.

INSTRUCTIONAL DECISIONS	CONNECTIONS TO UDL GUIDELINES
Develop flexible assessments: Students had a choice to write a constructed response, create a paper graphic organizer, or a digital graphic organizer. Students had options to do an oral presentation, create a poster, or do a mock interview in pairs.	UDL Guideline 5: Provide options for expression and communication. 5.1 Use multiple media for communication. 5.2 Use multiple tools for construction and composition. UDL Guideline 7: Provide options for recruiting interest. 7.1 Optimize individual choice and autonomy.
Use flexible methods: Teachers modeled compare/contrast activity with the whole class (provided modeling and guided practice through team teaching). Students worked in two smaller groups to discuss their opinions on the scenes that were changed (provided guided practice in parallel teaching).	UDL Guideline 3: Provide options for comprehension. 3.1 Activate or supply background knowledge. 3.2 Highlight patterns, critical features, big ideas, and relationships. UDL Guideline 6: Provide options for executive functions. 6.1 Guide appropriate goal-setting. 6.2 Support planning and strategy development. 6.3 Facilitate managing information and resources. 6.4 Enhance capacity for monitoring progress. UDL Guideline 7: Provide options for recruiting interest. 7.1 Optimize individual choice and autonomy. 7.2 Optimize relevance, value, and authenticity. UDL Guideline 8: Provide options for sustaining effort and persistence. 8.1 Heighten salience of goals and objectives. 8.2 Vary demands and resources to optimize challenge. 8.3 Foster collaboration and community. 8.4 Increase mastery-oriented feedback.

INSTRUCTIONAL DECISIONS	CONNECTIONS TO UDL GUIDELINES
Use flexible materials:	UDL Guideline1: Provide options for perception.
Use closed caption version of the movie.	1.2 Offer alternatives for auditory information.
	1.3 Offer alternatives for visual information.
Use read aloud/text-to-speech options for excerpts of the book.	UDL Guideline 4: Provide options for physical action.
	4.1 Vary the methods for response and navigation.
Offer options to create graphic organizers and posters.	4.2 Optimize access to tools and assistive technologies.
	UDL Guideline 5: Provide options for expression and communication.
	5.1 Use multiple media for communication.
	5.2 Use multiple tools for construction and composition.

Section 3

UDL Implementation in School Systems

8

Scaling the Work: A Small District Perspective

Rhonda J. Laswell, George Van Horn,
Tina Greene, Jessica Vogel, and Angie Wieneke

GUIDING QUESTIONS

- What specific steps should a district take to guide the implementation of Universal Design for Learning (UDL)?

- What do the phases of UDL implementation look like in a small district?

In this chapter, the authors describe the steps taken by the Bartholomew Consolidated School Corporation (BCSC) throughout the process of implementing UDL at the district level. They also explain how UDL became the district framework for curricula and instruction for all students. Finally, they share the actions taken, data collected, and tools used in the process.

INTRODUCTION TO BCSC

Bartholomew Consolidated School Corporation is nestled in the small midwestern city of Columbus in southcentral Indiana. It serves more than 12,000 students throughout Bartholomew County, which has a population of just over 80,000 and a median household income of $54,165. Twelve percent of the population lives at or below the poverty line. The county's ethnic makeup is as follows: White non-Hispanic, 84.6 percent; Hispanic/Latino, 6.4 percent; Asian, 5.4 percent; Black/African American, 2.3 percent; multiracial, 1.5 percent; American Indian/Alaskan Native, 0.5 percent; and Native Hawaiian/Other Pacific Islander, 0.1 percent.

BCSC's students are served on 18 campuses—eleven elementary schools, three high schools, two middle schools, one residential school, and one adult education center. Nearly 10 percent of BCSC students speak a language other than English in their home; 15 percent have limited English proficiency. Nearly 25 percent of BCSC students identify as minority, and they represent 54 different languages; 44.2 percent receive free and reduced-price lunch; 11.7 percent are identified to receive special education services, and 85 percent of those so identified spend at least 80 percent of their instruction time in the general education setting. The BCSC graduation rate is 89.1 percent; 27.2 percent of the residents have a bachelor's degree or higher.

BCSC's journey with UDL began well over a decade ago. During the 2002–2003 school year, BCSC initiated its exploration of UDL with a service-delivery plan that had a special education focus, which was married the following year with a technology-focused action plan. However, BCSC would be the first to say that neither technology nor special education should be the driving force behind the implementation of UDL. UDL is a belief system, a philosophy about teaching and learning that is deeply rooted in research-based neuroscience. The UDL framework guides all decision making at BCSC and is the district's framework for all curriculum and instruction for all students. This chapter discusses the actions taken, the data collected, and the tools used during BCSC's UDL implementation journey.

THE PROCESS

UDL implementation is a recursive process that requires those involved to revisit ongoing initiatives until UDL has become the framework through which all other initiatives are filtered. CAST describes UDL implementation as systemic change with five clearly defined phases: explore, prepare, integrate, scale, and optimize (National Center on Universal Design for Learning, 2012). Although CAST had not yet developed the UDL implementation process when BCSC first became involved, it is clear in retrospect that the district progressed through each phase of implementation as they are now defined.

Exploration and a Need for Change

BCSC became interested in the UDL framework when it was looking for a way to change how instruction was delivered to its students with special needs. This change was initially reflected in a service-delivery plan the district developed to provide an inclusive learning environment that met the needs of all students in the least restrictive environment. This emphasis on inclusion was the catalyst for a self-reflective process that led the district to UDL.

As an initial step in learning about instructional practices and decision making at BCSC, each school was given the opportunity to participate in facilitated meetings that focused on instructional planning for students with disabilities. In collaboration with the Center on Lifelong Learning, a center within the Indiana Institute on Disability at Indiana University, schools were asked to analyze their instructional decision-making process for students with disabilities. The outcome was a plan of action to ensure that the decisions made would support inclusive services for all students. BCSC also formed a partnership with PATINS, a statewide project in Indiana that focused on UDL and assistive technology and was selecting schools to serve as pilot sites over a period of several years.

The six BCSC schools selected as pilot sites participated in a study of the book *Teaching Every Student in the Digital Age: Universal Design for Learning* by David Rose and Anne Meyer (2002) from CAST. Each school developed a plan that focused on UDL and the various technologies that would support its implementation. They also reviewed the service-delivery plan for special education and began to set the stage for a district-wide special services delivery plan. The schools reported data from their UDL-focused technology plans to the PATINS project coordinator. It is important to note that UDL is often associated with technology, assistive technology, and special education. BCSC recognized this as a potential stumbling block and was careful to ensure that the pilot schools remained focused on UDL as a framework to support all learners. This deeper dive into learning about UDL, which BCSC had initiated to change practice in its schools, began to transform and change the district's knowledge and beliefs about teaching and learning for all.

As a result of the pilot school effort, teachers and school leaders began to see that what works for those in the margins often works better for everyone. A paradigm shift in thinking slowly began to occur, but not without some cognitive dissonance. It became evident that focusing only on students with disabilities and only on technology supports for one subgroup of students was perpetuating the student deficit model. BCSC leaders thus began to focus on moving from a student deficit model to practices that proactively removed barriers to learning. They began to view the environment as disabled, rather than the students, which was another critical turning point for teachers and leaders.

During this initial exploration stage, BCSC also began to consider how the UDL framework could impact student behavior. This question led to the introduction of Positive Behavioral Interventions and Supports (PBIS) as an optional initiative. The U.S. Department of Education's Office of Special Education Programs (2017) defines PBIS as a means to:

> ...define, develop, implement, and evaluate a multi-tiered approach to Technical Assistance that improves the capacity of states, districts and schools to establish, scale-up and sustain the PBIS framework. Emphasis is given to the impact of implementing PBIS on the social, emotional and academic outcomes for students with disabilities.

After the discussion about behavior, BCSC decided to apply for a federal grant to develop school-wide PBIS systems for each school in the district. In partnership with the Center on Lifelong Learning, BCSC applied for and received a federal grant to fund a year of planning and developing school-wide PBIS systems in all seventeen BCSC schools. Again, as BCSC's beliefs and knowledge about behavior were challenged, current practices were evaluated and revised to align with PBIS. All seventeen schools created PBIS action plans as the district entered the next phase of UDL implementation.

> ### A Teacher's Perspective
>
> UDL implementation is all about developing meaningful lessons and creating a productive classroom environment. Education should be designed to prepare students for the real world. UDL helps us to achieve this goal. Students become enthusiastic learners, goal-oriented citizens, and knowledgeable individuals. By implementing the UDL principles, I can teach them how to be resourceful and how important it is for them to take responsibility for their own learning.
>
> —KALEIGH MCKILLIAN, middle school teacher

Preparation

During the preparation phase of UDL implementation, the district leadership began to view UDL as a framework to support focused, systemic change. As they reflected on the district's reforms, they recognized that many of their worthwhile initiatives were only random improvement efforts. They realized that they needed a conceptual framework to tie these efforts together, and soon determined that UDL should be the framework through which all other initiatives could be filtered. At the time, the district had completed a white-paper on learning in the twenty-first century, a document intended to guide their strategic planning, and they quickly realized that UDL had to be a significant component of their conceptual framework. BCSC developed a clear focus during this time of transition, and the leadership agreed to do the following:

- Create a climate that was flexible and maintained high expectations for all.

- Map resources and processes specific to personnel, structures such as planning time, materials, curriculum, and professional development.

- Define a strategic vision and plan of action with expected outcomes.

As a result, many "random acts of improvement" (see Figure 8.1) were evaluated and aligned within a cohesive framework. UDL moved from being thought of as an initiative to being "the" framework through which all other initiatives were filtered. To develop understanding at the building level, each school was asked to create a team that would integrate the UDL framework into their planning process. These teams consisted of teachers and staff members who set goals related to teacher training and increasing UDL implementation in the classroom. These teams received professional development from district staff who had expertise in UDL. The teams were strongly encouraged to embed the UDL goals in their school improvement plans. BCSC also began to conduct measures of school-wide UDL understanding.

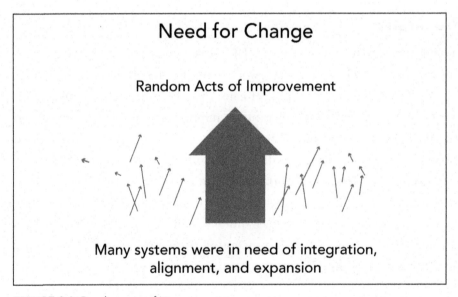

FIGURE 8.1 Random act of improvement

At the same time, PBIS became a district-wide initiative and systems were implemented in all seventeen schools. PBIS coaches, facilitators, and teams were established to service and support all BCSC campuses. The district collected and evaluated monthly PBIS data to look for disproportionalities, such as over-representation of students receiving special education services, and also conducted annual school evaluations of the PBIS implementation. Over time, PBIS took on a different meaning at BCSC than it did in the national literature; as the district moved to the instructional piece of PBIS that supports the implementation of UDL, it changed the "I" from meaning "intervention" to meaning "instruction." BCSC leaders felt this emphasized the importance of teaching student behavior and creating instructional options for all students. This subtle yet impactful change in verbiage supported the UDL framework as it applies to behavior.

The wheels of change had begun to turn. A major paradigm shift had begun, and pockets of excellence were taking root in classrooms across the district. Although the trend was positive, district leadership quickly learned that managing such complex change would be a slow and arduous task that often manifested in confusion, anxiety, resistance, frustration, and false starts (Ambrose, 1987). They also realized that, to truly move forward from UDL exploration and preparation, school leaders and teachers alike would need to examine and self-reflect on their beliefs, knowledge, and practices.

Integration

As BCSC moved to a more clearly defined integration of UDL, each teacher in the district received the UDL self-assessment rubric (Figure 8.2) to help them reflect on their knowledge of UDL and its implementation in their learning environments. The rubric was created by Bill Jensen, BCSC's director of secondary education, and Jessica Vogel, assistant director of special education. Jensen and Vogel used CAST's UDL principles and Guidelines to create the nonevaluative rubric that was used to collect data about areas where professional development was needed. Each school in the district was responsible for collecting and disseminating these data, which helped to identify training needs.

UDL Principle	UDL Teaching Method	Not Yet Evident	Emerging	Intermediate	Advanced
Multiple means of representation	Provide multiple examples	Students are only given one example of skills needed to complete the assignment.	In preparation for a lesson, the teacher has few examples that identify skills and concepts needed to complete the assignment.	In preparation for a lesson, the teacher creates some examples to find and identify skills and concepts needed to complete the assignment.	In preparation for a lesson, the **teacher and students** create multiple examples of finding and identifying skills and concepts needed to complete the assignment.
Multiple means of representation	Highlight critical features	Teacher provides critical information for the lesson through only one modality.	Teacher provides critical information for the lesson through only two modalities.	The teacher provides critical information for the lesson through oral and visual presentation and highlights critical features in written and visual form, then monitors students to check their focus on important features of the lesson.	The teacher provides critical information for the lesson through oral and visual presentation and highlights critical features in written and visual form, then monitors students to check their focus on important features of the lesson. Additionally, by having texts available in digital format, the teacher or students could literally highlight critical features of the text while preparing the lesson assignments.

FIGURE 8.2 Part of a UDL self-assessment rubric for teachers and administrators. Download the full assessment at www.bcsc.k12.in.us/Page/10928.

As the need for professional development increased, BCSC decided to hire a part-time UDL consultant to broaden support for all the staff, from classroom teachers to administrators. The consultant, Loui Lord Nelson, was responsible for meeting with classroom teachers interested in guidance on meeting the variable needs of the students in their learning environments. Dr. Nelson was also tasked with providing professional development to school administrators and UDL committees. As the district worked to expand professional learning options related to UDL, it also began to take a closer look at inclusion across the district. Instructional consultation teams (ICTs) were developed to support teachers in the design and delivery of instruction for all learners. The ICTs' role was to respond to teachers' requests for reading, writing, math, and behavior support. This enabled teachers to collaborate with a member of the ICT in making an instructional match during classroom instruction and on specific tasks. This process focused on the learning environment and instructional strategies, not on the student, while supporting the foundations of UDL and giving teachers a process they could use to provide assistance and support.

BCSC teachers continued using the UDL self-assessment rubric, and the district found that, as the teachers learned more about UDL, they began to rate themselves lower on the self- assessment. After a few years of working with a consultant, requests for professional development and classroom observations continued to increase. It became clear that BCSC needed to evaluate the district's capacity to support teachers in the implementation of UDL.

A Teacher's Perspective

Now that I have immersed myself in UDL, I don't think I could ever teach in any setting without considering the Guidelines, consciously or subconsciously. I know UDL has made me a better educator of both students and adults. It's important to always remember that variability is the norm and disability is contextual. Implementing UDL takes a lot of intentional thought, planning, and hard work, but when you see the results and changes it produces, you will never go back!

—KATE EDGREN, UDL facilitator

Scaling

It eventually became clear that BCSC needed a full-time UDL coordinator. The position was approved, giving the district a full-time employee dedicated to UDL professional development for teachers and district administrators. The UDL coordinator began working with the district's ICT coordinator to train the ICT facilitators at each school. The facilitators in turn supported the teachers in each building, which they did with the UDL framework and PBIS in mind.

Again, the wheels of change began to turn. Prior beliefs, knowledge, and practice were brought into question as BCSC began to fully integrate PBIS into the work of the district's ICT coordinator and the building level ICT facilitators. As a result, the connections between the IC process and PBIS began to take their place under the UDL framework. Thinking outside the box about behavior allowed BCSC to avoid the use of tiers. BCSC believed that focusing on positive behavior instructional supports applied in conjunction with UDL, rather than on tiers connected to student failure, would create a predictable environment that balanced structure and variety. The gap between what a student expects and what really happens in the classroom can cause stress, anxiety, and misbehavior. In contrast, a safe, predictable environment with accessible learning options fosters engagement and risk-taking is needed so that students are encouraged, empowered, and inspired to become expert learners. Using the UDL framework to evaluate its students' behavior, BCSC made a comparison between traditional discipline systems and PBIS (see Table 8.1).

TABLE 8.1 BCSC's comparison between traditional discipline systems and PBIS

PBIS	TRADITIONAL DISCIPLINE
Proactive	Reactive
Evaluates environment, classroom, culture	Evaluates the student
Intentional	Cause/effect
Designs procedures and protocols before Students arrive	Reiterates what behavior is *not* appropriate
Focuses on variability	Focuses on individual behavior
Plans for the margins	Plans for the illusionary "average"
Values variety	Conforms to "normal"
Removes barriers	Works around barriers
Positive	Negative
Expectations are known	Expectations are hidden

As BCSC began to scale UDL implementation and expand its structures to support the ongoing process, it moved seamlessly and systematically from one phase of UDL implementation to the next.

During this next phase, BCSC became better able to promote professional growth by supporting a UDL community of practice that was responsive to individual and system variability. Effective practices, processes, and structures were expanded through professional development and technical assistance, whereas the schools continued to identify specific training needs related to UDL implementation.

Using the CAST self-assessment rubric, BCSC continued to reflect on UDL implementation. As barriers were identified, the UDL coordinator and district administrators began working to remove them. The state was adopting a teacher-evaluation model known as RISE, but school districts were given the option to use RISE or to create their own evaluation system; because BCSC was so deeply invested in UDL, it chose to create its own. The UDL consultant, UDL coordinator, teacher union representatives, and district administrators worked together to create the evaluation, in which the UDL implementation counted for 50 percent of a teacher's evaluation. The teacher evaluation rubric was then piloted at one elementary, one middle, and one high school during the 2013–2014 school year.

As of 2017, the revised rubric continues to support both the implementation and the sustainability of UDL at BCSC (Figure 8.3). It is also used to guide reflective conversations, promote intentional practice, and set goals around UDL, and provides a foundation for ongoing professional growth throughout the entire district around UDL, PBIS, academic citizenship, and student achievement, performance, and growth.

BCSC 2014-15 TEACHER SUCCESS RUBRIC		TEACHER BEING EVALUATED		
			EVALUATOR	
	INEFFECTIVE (1)	NEEDS IMPROVEMENT (2)	EFFECTIVE (3)	HIGHLY EFFECTIVE (4)
INSTRUCTIONAL FRAMEWORK — UDL	€ The goal is not posted	€ The goal is posted but not addressed or instructional methods are not aligned with the goal	€ The goal is posted and instructional methods and materials align with the goal	€ The goal is posted, attainable and accessible. Instructional methods and materials align with the goal
	€ Potential barriers are not considered during the planning of the lesson or the design of the learning environment	€ Potential barriers are considered but the teacher is not applying that knowledge to the lesson plan	€ Potential barriers are considered and the teacher applies that knowledge to the learning environment	€ Potential barriers in the curriculum and learning environment are identified and addressed in the design of the lesson and the learning environment
	€ Content and skills are presented without options and scaffolding	€ Content is presented with few options and skills are presented without scaffolding	€ Content and skills are presented in multiple ways with options but with minimal scaffolding	€ Content and skills are presented in multiple ways with options and scaffolding available
	€ Students are not engaged	€ Students are engaged in relevant learning opportunities	€ Students are engaged in relevant and meaningful learning opportunities	€ Students are engaged in authentic, relevant, and meaningful learning opportunities
	€ Students do not interact with or demonstrate content and skill comprehension	€ Students interact with content and skill comprehension but do not demonstrate knowledge	€ Students interact with and demonstrate content and skill comprehension in multiple ways	€ Students consistently interact with and demonstrate content and skill comprehension in multiple ways

FIGURE 8.3A Teacher evaluation rubric

BCSC
2014-15 DEAN/COUNSELOR SUCCESS RUBRIC

DEAN/COUNSELOR BEING EVALUATED

EVALUATOR

		INEFFECTIVE (1)	NEEDS IMPROVEMENT (2)	EFFECTIVE (3)	HIGHLY EFFECTIVE (4)
INSTRUCTIONAL FRAMEWORK	UDL	€ School wide goals are not known	€ School wide goals are known but not addressed or instructional resources are not aligned with the goals	€ School wide goals are known and instructional resources align with the goal	€ School wide goals are known, attainable and accessible. Instructional resources align with the goal
		€ Potential barriers are not considered during the planning of the interaction or the design of the learning environment	€ Potential barriers are considered but the building administrator is not applying that knowledge to the interaction	€ Potential barriers are considered and the building administrator applies that knowledge to the learning environment	€ Potential barriers related to the resources, information, and learning environment are identified and addressed in the design of the interaction and the learning environment
		€ Content and skills are presented without options and scaffolding	€ Content is presented with few options and skills are presented without scaffolding	€ Content and skills are presented in multiple ways with options but with minimal scaffolding	€ Content and skills are presented in multiple ways with options and scaffolding available
		€ The students and/or parents are not engaged	€ The students and/or parents are engaged in relevant learning opportunities	€ The students and/or parents are engaged in relevant and meaningful learning opportunities	€ The students and/or parents are engaged in authentic, relevant, and meaningful learning opportunities
		€ The students do not demonstrate and articulate appropriate choices	€ The students rarely demonstrate and articulate appropriate choices	€ The students occasionally demonstrate and articulate appropriate choices	€ The students consistently demonstrate and articulate appropriate choices

FIGURE 8.3B Dean/Counselor Success Rubric

BCSC
2014-15 BUILDING ADMINISTRATOR SUCCESS RUBRIC

ADMINISTRATOR BEING EVALUATED

EVALUATOR

		INEFFECTIVE (1)	NEEDS IMPROVEMENT (2)	EFFECTIVE (3)	HIGHLY EFFECTIVE (4)
INSTRUCTIONAL FRAMEWORK	UDL	€ School wide goals are not known	€ School wide goals are known but not addressed or instructional resources are not aligned with the goals	€ School wide goals are known and instructional resources align with the goal	€ School wide goal are known, attainable, and accessible. Instructional resources align with the goal
		€ Potential barriers are not considered during the planning of the interaction or the design of the learning environment	€ Potential barriers are considered but the building administrator is not applying that knowledge to the interaction	€ Potential barriers are considered and the building administrator applies that knowledge to the learning environment	€ Potential barriers related to the resources, information and learning environment are identified and addressed in the design of the interaction and the learning environment
		€ Content and skills are presented without options and scaffolding	€ Content is presented with few options and skills are presented without scaffolding	€ Content and skills are presented in multiple ways with options but with minimal scaffolding	€ Content and skills are presented in multiple ways with options and scaffolding available
		€ The school community members are not engaged	€ The school community members are engaged in relevant learning opportunities	€ The school community members are engaged in relevant and meaningful learning opportunities	€ The school community members are engaged in authentic, relevant and meaningful learning opportunities
		€ The school community members do not interact with or demonstrate content and skill comprehension	€ The school community members interact with content and skill comprehension but do not demonstrate knowledge	€ The school community members interact with and demonstrate content and skill comprehension in multiple ways	€ The school community members consistently interact with and demonstrate content and skill comprehension in multiple ways

FIGURE 8.3C Building Administrator Evaluation Rubric

A Teacher's Perspective

The biggest challenge in implementing Universal Design for Learning is the conceptual shift. This requires us to commit to being uncomfortable. You have to start asking, "Why am I doing what I do? How does this remove barriers to learning? How does this relate to the learning objective?" Discomfort is good. That's what growth feels like.

—JONI DEGNER, UDL Facilitator

A Student's Perspective

One of my favorite classes in high school was English with Mr. D. I [usually] hated English, so why was this my favorite class? Well, it was because he used UDL in his classroom every day. This involved "trailer Tuesday," which pulled together the overall lessons for the week while tying them to a movie with the same theme. He also used a variety of activities involving hands-on, visuals, and verbal components to benefit all of his students simultaneously. UDL helped me be excited to learn. What more could you want students to feel before coming to class?

—EMMA L., BCSC graduate

Optimize

As we moved into the optimization phase, BCSC was fully invested in UDL as the curriculum framework. The district recognized the importance of aligning district initiatives (PBIS, ICT), so BCSC changed the ICT coordinator job into that of the UDL coordinator, who also supported PBIS and ICT. The CAST district assessment tool created a desire for more support and professional development around the use of technology in the learning environment, which led BCSC to change the role of district media specialist into the UDL coordinator, and to focus on instructional media technology.

As BCSC's successful pilot of the teacher evaluation rubric was expanded to the entire district, data from the evaluations were reviewed. With 50 percent of the rubric evaluating the implementation of UDL in the learning environment, BCSC recognized the need to have the ICT facilitators become UDL facilitators who would both support teachers' requests for help in reading, writing, math, and behavior, and help them align their strategies, instruction, and learning environment through the UDL lens. Teachers' "requests for assistance" from the UDL facilitators thus became "requests for educational planning." The teacher evaluation rubric continues to be instrumental in guiding professional development, which is based on data obtained annually.

A Teacher's Perspective

My greatest successes with UDL would have to be in student engagement. I grew up with history classes that were snooze city—"read this section and answer the questions at the end." As a history teacher myself, I knew I didn't want to take that approach, but I had no idea how much UDL would help me engage my students. I can't count the number of times I've had students say, "This is my favorite class and I've always hated history." I put a lot of attention and detail into my lesson plans, and it completely pays off when I see how interested the kids get.

—MOLLY FOUNTAIN, middle school teacher

PROFESSIONAL LEARNING OPTIONS

BCSC offers a variety of professional learning options for its staff, from in-school professional development to summer conferences. As the district moved forward in aligning its various initiatives, leaders realized that classroom teachers would benefit from having just one way to request assistance.

This led to the development of the request for educational planning form (see Figure 8.4), which allows teachers to request help in planning for UDL, ICT, PBIS, special education evaluation, technology, and so forth. Being able to pick one of the various types of support available using a single document has streamlined such requests. Many BCSC schools have also developed professional learning communities to support professional development around the principles and Guidelines of UDL, as well as the characteristics of the expert learner. These professional learning communities were created by building administrators with support from the UDL facilitators, which has helped to lead these communities as a support to teachers.

Request for Educational Planning

Date Submitted:

Teacher name: Grade: If Secondary Level, course name:

Specific Request:

Check all that apply (Learning Environment Design is required for all requests)

- ☐ UDL
- ☐ PBIS
- ☐ ICT
- ☐ Technology (specific to instructional use)
- ☐ Literacy - Specify: ☐ reading ☐ writing
- ☐ Math
- ☐ Behavior
- ☐ Special Education Evaluation (**Student Information Form required**)

  If this is a request for a Special Education Evaluation, please submit to the building administrator. All other requests may be given to the UDL Facilitator or UDL Instructional Coach.

Revised: August, 2014   Page 1

FIGURE 8.4 Request for educational planning form

Policy has also driven the design of professional learning at BCSC. Indiana legislation has mandated that schools collect data on student growth for nontested content areas. BCSC administrators dedicated many brainstorming sessions to choosing a measurement tool for its students. Their conversations on UDL and CAST's characteristics of an expert learner enabled them to create school-wide learning outcomes (SWLOs) that were based on the CAST characteristics. Schools piloted the SWLOs and collected data based on the SWLO rubric, which is used by all BCSC schools. Data obtained using the rubric help drive staff professional development. Many UDL facilitators have recently worked with classroom teachers to create lessons for students about the characteristics of expert learners, which explain how a student can become an expert learner.

BCSC also has developed a UDL summer institute that provides high-quality, intensive learning opportunities that are aligned with district priorities. BCSC sees this weeklong exploration into UDL as an opportunity to focus on and model the framework in practice. The structure of the overall institute and the individual sessions is designed to model multiple means of engagement, representation, action, and expression. For example, institute leaders collect daily feedback from the teachers and visitors, and adjust the following day's sessions. Each summer institute has a theme, such as learning environment design or the characteristics of an expert learner, which guides the conversation and the development of products created by participants throughout the week. The institute, which has completed its fourth year, continues to provide an exceptional learning experience for all staff, from administrators to newly hired teachers to seasoned staff who return each year to build on their knowledge of UDL.

A Parent's Perspective

For me, UDL provides teachers with an instructional framework that allows my child to partipcate in the general education classroom. He is able to learn the grade-level standards with age-appropriate peers. By empowering teachers to instruct my child, and many different levels of children, he has more opportunities to grow and a more promising future. My child will only get one education, and I feel more hopeful with the use of UDL in the classroom.

—CRISTY MCARDLE, parent of a BCSC student

CONCLUSION

Nearing the end of its first decade of UDL implementation, BCSC's commitment to the framework remains strong, and it is now the curriculum and instruction framework for all BCSC students. The district has also begun to focus on creating school-wide learning outcomes based on the CAST characteristics of expert learners. BCSC has been recognized nationally as a leader in UDL implementation, most recently as a featured district in the 2016 National Education Technology Plan, which highlighted the district's UDL implementation as a model of best practice in teaching and learning. As the district works to scale and optimize its UDL implementation, it has established partnerships with local businesses and institutes of higher education, which has strengthened application of the framework, not only in the schools but in the community. Although pleased with the progress made so far, BCSC continues to develop new ways to innovate and apply the UDL framework in practice, all while focusing on developing learners who are knowledgeable, resourceful, strategic, goal-directed, motivated, and purposeful.

9

Universal Design for Learning: Building Learner-Centered Environments in a Large District

William Burke

GUIDING QUESTION

- How does a large school district incorporate the Universal Design for Learning (UDL) framework into its strategic plan?

This chapter provides an overview of the Baltimore County Public Schools (BCPS) strategic plan for communication, professional development, and stakeholder buy-in about UDL. It also highlights the eight changes—we call them "conversions"—that must be considered by any district planning to adopt a large-scale UDL initiative.

INTRODUCTION TO BCPS

The Baltimore County Public Schools (BCPS) currently serve more than 111,000 students and employ nearly 9,000 teachers. To change teacher practice, and ultimately student outcomes, on such a large scale, BCPS engages in explicit strategic-planning processes. This chapter is designed to walk you through the BCPS process for implementing a large-scale initiative designed to change teacher practice through professional learning. This work aims to improve student achievement by providing access to curriculum and instruction that address learner variability through personalization and customization.

Over the past thirty years, BCPS has experienced a dramatic demographic shift. A once predominantly white student body has become a minority-majority student body. The share of students receiving free and reduced-price meals has increased from less than 10 percent of the student body to nearly 50 percent. The number of homeless students and students for whom English is a second language is increasing at similar rates. As a result of these changing demographics, BCPS is experiencing gaps in student performance. When students have different experiences based on their cultural backgrounds, they also often have different perceptions and ways of processing information (Chita-Tegmark, Gravel, Serpa, Domings, & Rose, 2012), a fact that must be considered when planning instruction.

We also have learned that participation in advanced academics and special education, and academic success, can be predicted using racial and socio-economic data. BCPS is determined to give students the opportunity to be globally competitive regardless of their cultural background or socioeconomic status, and to raise the bar for all students while closing achievement gaps. The UDL framework is a powerful tool that researchers and educators are more widely recognizing as an effective means to respond to individual differences. Eleven of twelve research articles analyzed by Al-Azawei, Serenelli, and Lundqvist (2016) in their literature review found that UDL implementation has a positive impact, thus emphasizing the importance and benefits of a large-scale implementation.

STRATEGIC PLANNING FOR LARGE-SCALE CHANGE INITIATIVES

Adopting UDL fundamentally changed teaching and learning at BCPS. The district developed a strategic-planning framework that included eight conversions that any district planning to adopt a large-scale initiative must consider (see Figure 9.1). The conversions are:

- Curriculum

- Instruction

- Assessment

- Professional learning

- Infrastructure

- Policy

- Budget

- Communication

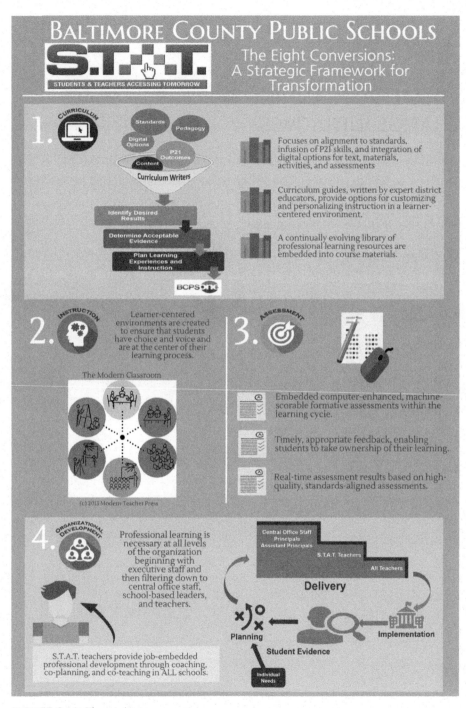

FIGURE 9.1A The eight conversations

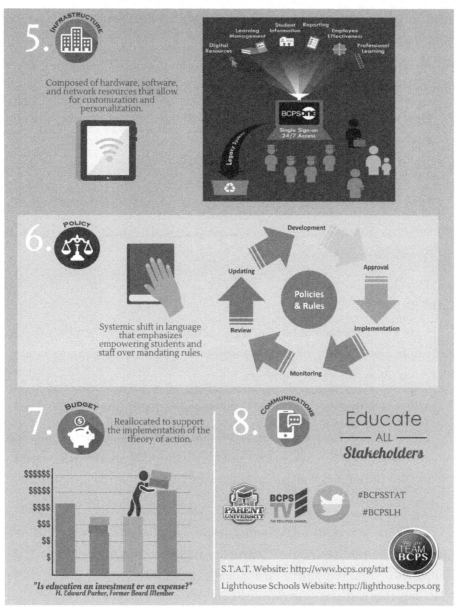

FIGURE 9.1B The eight conversations

The Eight Conversions: A Strategic Framework for Transformation

We encourage districts to consider the following questions when determining how to embed UDL in teacher practice most successfully:

- How should curriculum be designed to remove barriers to teaching and learning?

- What must change in how teachers deliver instruction?

- How do assessments inform personalized and customized learning?

- Which stakeholders need to receive professional learning before they will be able to maximize support?

Curriculum

If teachers are expected to use the UDL guiding principles when they design and implement lessons, the principles must be embedded in the curriculum. BCPS has done this in the following ways:

- All curriculum writers receive professional learning about UDL.

- The templates for lesson-plan development and unit maps contain sections that direct teachers to low-tech and high-tech resources that account for and respond to learner variability. BCPS calls this the customization and personalization of curriculum.

Teachers' access to high-quality resources that guide them in developing lessons that respond to learner variability are critical to the UDL implementation. Without such resources embedded in the curriculum, UDL becomes just one more initiative that adds to teachers' workload. Curriculum guides are just that—guides—and they should include examples of UDL teaching practices for new teachers or teachers new to UDL. They also should provide exemplars that enable teachers to draw on their professional knowledge and exercise autonomy when creating lessons based on their students' needs.

Embedding UDL resources in the curriculum guides also ensures that teachers are using approved resources that align with curriculum standards. Providing digital tools and resources that are approved and embedded in the curriculum also ensures that data-sharing and student privacy issues are addressed and controlled by the district.

Instruction

BCPS uses the term "effective first instruction" to describe lessons that consider learner variability in the planning process. Building lessons that offer students multiple supports and modes of access aligns with a growth mindset learning model, in which teachers believe students can develop intelligence. In a deficit model, teachers intervene only after they determine what a student doesn't know and provide supports only after a student has not succeeded. Teachers who adopt a growth mindset model work to identify potential instructional barriers and then address gaps in learning while building on students' existing knowledge.

At BCPS, we have worked to develop student-centered instruction, which recognizes that all students are unique in their preferences, needs, and abilities, which impacts their learning experience (Al-Azawei et al., 2016). Student-centered instruction also provides access to a curriculum that is adaptive and responsive to learner variability, that gives students choice and voice and that puts them at the center of the learning environment. When planning and delivering these lessons, teachers consider learner variability first. This is observed in classrooms where multiple pathways are the norm. Having multiple, flexible groups of students enables teachers to build foundational skills and address rigorous comprehension standards in the same lesson. Scaffolding lessons with support makes it possible for all learners to access grade-level content.

BCPS One is an online learning-management system that gives students multiple learning activities, offers formative assessments to determine student proficiency, and customizes curriculum resources to each student's proficiency level. These multiple learning activities are grounded in the UDL principles to provide multiple means of representation, multiple means of action and expression, and multiple means of engagement (CAST, 2011; Rose & Meyer, 2002). Students personalize their learning by choosing the instructional activities that give them the support and access they need to meet curriculum standards. This scaffolding supports all students, not only those who have disabilities and/or cultural differences (Chita-Tegmark et al., 2012). The increased formative assessment data also help teachers make more informed decisions about future instruction.

Assessment

Teachers often struggle to provide assessment options because student achievement ultimately will be assessed using standardized tests. They worry that if they give their students assessment choices the children won't be able to translate their learning when it's time to take a standardized test. There is a compromise. Providing assessments that are based on students' learning needs as well as those that mirror standardized testing formats throughout the learning cycle will give students access to rigorous content while providing practice in common testing formats.

BCPS uses formative assessments to measure progress in daily instruction and summative assessments at the end of learning units to measure how learning progress aligns with curriculum standards. Formative assessments designed using the UDL Guidelines and principles can uncover more of what students really know because they enable students to choose the option that maximizes their ability to share their learning. Formative assessments provide important data that help teachers plan subsequent lessons more effectively because they can be clear about what students know. Formative assessments and feedback drive the development of personalized instruction for students, ensure that instruction is appropriate and effective for each student, and ensure that barriers to learning are considered in the lesson plan development, not in response to deficits.

Summative assessments provide important data on student learning, as well as opportunities to measure student progress against standards benchmarks. Summative assessments are best used as evidence when assigning grades. Although formative assessments align more closely with the UDL principles, the principles also can be considered when preparing for summative assessments. The UDL checkpoints that relate to reducing emotional threats and distractions and supporting executive function are important when preparing students for standardized assessments. The framework reminds teachers to provide models that help students know what to expect on an assessment and give them strategies for deconstructing standardized assessment items. In both instances, the UDL framework can help teachers identify barriers and provide all learners with supports and scaffolds.

Professional Learning

The power of professional learning is maximized when the instructional activities model effective teaching practices. When preparing professional development on UDL, presenters should model multiple means of engagement, representation, action, and expression, and ensure that all resources are aligned with the framework. When teachers engage in professional learning activities that clearly address learner variability, they begin to see the value of teaching with the UDL framework. Experiencing UDL as a learner is one of the most powerful tools for encouraging educators to change their own teaching practices.

In addition to designing high-quality, universally designed professional development, a large district also needs to consider how to effectively communicate their work to teachers. There are two essential questions to ask when considering professional learning needs: Who needs to learn the information first? What supports are needed to move staff through the stages of UDL implementation?

When developing a professional learning rollout plan, BCPS determines in what order district, administrative, and school staff will receive training, based on the support each group needs for effective implementation. For example, assistant superintendents are the first to receive professional learning because they provide guidance and support to the administrators they evaluate. Principals and assistant principals receive professional learning next because they guide and support all staff. Coaches or professional development teachers, who guide and support teachers, are the next to receive professional learning, and teachers receive professional learning when the appropriate support staff have been trained and have the resources to offer them effective on-the-job professional learning. Table 9.1 provides an example of topics and audiences for professional learning about UDL.

TABLE 9.1: Professional learning timeline

	ASSISTANT SUPERINTENDENTS	PRINCIPALS AND ASSISTANT PRINCIPALS	COACHES OR PROFESSIONAL DEVELOPMENT TEACHERS	TEACHERS
Month 1	Explore: What is UDL?			
Month 2	Prepare: UDL resources to support teaching and learning in BCPS	Explore: What is UDL?		
Month 3	Integrate: Curriculum implementation	Prepare: UDL resources to support teaching and learning in BCPS	Explore: What is UDL?	
Month 4	Scale: Coaching	Integrate: Curriculum implementation	Prepare: UDL resources to support teaching and learning in BCPS	Explore: What is UDL?
Month 5	Optimize: Feedback for continuous improvement	Scale: Coaching	Integrate: Curriculum implementation	Prepare: UDL resources to support teaching and learning in BCPS
Month 6		Optimize: Feedback for continuous improvement	Scale: Coaching	Integrate: Curriculum implementation
Month 7			Optimize: Feedback for continuous improvement	

The early road to UDL implementation at BCPS was paved with one-shot workshops that focused on foundational knowledge, and the district was essentially stuck in the exploration stage for almost a decade; large-scale change in teacher practice was never realized (see Figure 9.2 for a visual representation of this process). The real shift toward UDL integration occurred when BCPS engaged in a grant project with CAST that involved implementing UDL at two middle schools. The project focused on job-embedded learning, with coaches providing support around resources and application. Teachers worked to design instruction using the UDL principles and formed a professional learning community (PLC) that met monthly to share resources and ideas, triumphs, and barriers—and to celebrate successes.

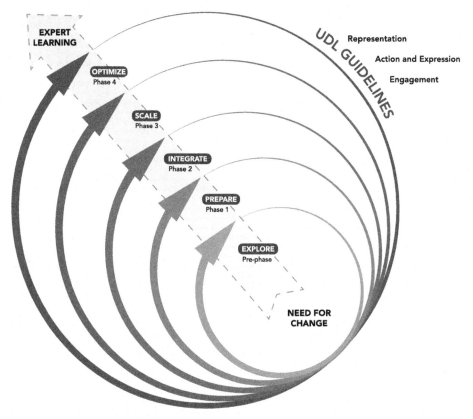

FIGURE 9.2 Phases of UDL implementation

The participating teachers completed a three-credit professional learning course on UDL and instruction that enabled them to develop proficiency using the resources and guiding principles of UDL. Due to the positive results, when the grant ended the BCPS office of professional development and Towson University committed to extend the project. They allocated funds to continue job-embedded coaching and for teacher stipends so those involved in the PLC could meet after school. This process taught BCPS some essential lessons in how to move teachers from exploration to integration. The success of the project was attributed to the PLCs and to the coaches who supported teachers as they learned the principles of UDL.

Communication

UDL is a central part of effective first instruction. It gives all students daily access to learning that is rigorous, relevant, accessible, and responsive. Therefore, it is important that UDL is not seen as just one more thing teachers must do. Our first step in communicating this message was to clarify the foundations of the district's teaching and learning framework. This framework has five main purposes:

1. Articulate the core beliefs of BCPS about teaching and learning.

2. Support the delivery of high-quality first instruction in *every* classroom to *every* child *every* day through a structured definition of the concept of "effective first instruction."

3. Develop the common language needed to facilitate conversations among administrators, teachers, parents, and students in regard to effective instructional practices.

4. Provide a consistent approach to monitoring teaching and learning while balancing the art and science of teaching.

5. Provide a framework to guide the priorities and work of the system—curriculum, professional development, program selection and evaluation, professional evaluation, budget, policy, infrastructure, etc.

The second step in communication was to embed UDL in the curriculum guidance documents. The final step was to align the written, taught, and assessed curriculums and provide professional learning that was explicit about using UDL in a blended learning environment.

MOVING FORWARD

When considering how to scale UDL most efficiently and effectively, districts are encouraged to consider the following questions:

- Are policies aligned to support the change, or do they create barriers?

- How can existing budgets be aligned or reallocated to support the initiative?

- What changes to buildings, classrooms, and networks are needed to support the change?

As we move forward with UDL implementation at BCPS, we must consider the impact that policy, budget, and infrastructure have on our work. Maryland is the first state to include UDL in its state education regulations (COMAR 13A.03.06). As a result, in the reports and plans for improvement required by the state, school districts provide evidence of their work in implementing the UDL Guidelines and principles. The state education department also encourages districts to use the UDL self-assessment rubric (see chapter 10 for additional information).

Evaluation of teachers and principals is also a topic of great importance. As evaluation models are refined and improved, including UDL is something to consider. If used effectively, evaluations support the growth of teachers and principals, but they also can influence employment decisions. Therefore, employee bargaining units must support any future evaluation that mandates UDL implementation.

Although UDL implementation does not require computer technology and a digital curriculum, there is no denying that assets such as computers, software applications, and other technological resources support the adaptations needed to meet learner variability. Technology offers another way to present information, can increase engagement, and can be a social equalizer (Pace & Blue, 2010). For example, the purchase of computers and digitized curriculum resources for BCPS students required redirecting budgets to support changes to the curriculum, instruction, and assessment that were associated with UDL implementation and personalized and customized learning.

To provide a digital curriculum and other assets that would be used by 8,800 teachers and 111,000 students, BCPS prioritized the procurement of hardware, software, and networks that could support this level of use. Without consistent equitable network access for all students, digital resources cannot support a flexible and responsive curriculum. BCPS policies for the procurement of curriculum resources thus require that physical copies of the resources be displayed for public review. Unlike hard copies of curriculum resources, digital curriculum resources can be updated instantaneously. Because digital resources play such a significant role in giving students responsive and adaptive instruction aligned with the Guidelines and principles of UDL, several policies needed to be reviewed and updated.

CONCLUSION: MONITORING FOR CONTINUOUS IMPROVEMENT

As with any large initiative, to refine and revise the UDL implementation at BCPS appropriately, it is important to monitor the outcomes. The goal of implementing UDL and student-centered teaching is equitable access to high-quality instruction that results in improved student achievement. To that end, BCPS monitored the following data:

- The number of teachers who received training on UDL and student centered teaching

- The use of digital resources by students

- Observational data on blended learning, small-group instruction, collaborative learning, and independent learning

- Teacher surveys on the effects of support from the school-based professional development teacher

- Student achievement as measured by the norm-referenced tests in math and reading given two or three times a year, depending on the grade

Based on the results of the data, BCPS continually adjusts the training it provides to teachers in order to support improved student learning.

BCPS believes that providing students with equitable access to rigorous and flexible curriculum and instruction that can be customized and personalized to address learner variability will improve student achievement. UDL is the foundation for that personalization and customization. Providing multiple means of representation, engagement, action, and expression in effective first instruction ensures that all students can learn and succeed at a high level.

10

Universal Design for Learning at the State Level: A Maryland State of Mind

Denise DeCoste, Marsye Kaplan, Elizabeth Berquist, Susan Spinnato, George D. Brown, and Christina J. Schindler

GUIDING QUESTIONS

- How can Universal Design for Learning (UDL) become part of state regulations?

- What is the state's role in the implementation of UDL?

- What does UDL look like in local school systems?

The purpose of this chapter is to describe how UDL became part of state regulations in Maryland and to identify how a state education department can support UDL implementation. This chapter also highlights the variability of UDL implementation in Maryland's local school systems.

REFLECTING ON THE JOURNEY

On a spring morning in 2016, leaders from the Maryland State Department of Education (MSDE) joined educators from across the nation on model site visits to two Maryland school systems as part of the Universal Design for Learning Implementation and Research Network annual summit. The walk-through schedule in each school allowed participants to observe a variety of classrooms.

When the MSDE colleagues reflected on the visits, they noted that the classrooms had varied as much as the learners and teachers. The physical aspects were unique and offered a wide array of flexible learning environments. Learners were able to articulate their goals, and flexibility in teacher presentations was evident in every classroom. Differentiated instruction planned with clear attention to scaffolding gave all students to access learning, and the learners were accustomed to having choices in how they gained information and showed what they knew. Cooperative and supportive learning was evident in all settings; the students looked to one another for support and feedback in an environment that encouraged mutual trust and respect. The children were confident, and they demonstrated high levels of interpersonal connection as they worked with and aided their peers during independent learning activities.

The diverse group of site visitors was impressed and inspired by the classes and was actively engaged in the planned reflection and information sessions with the schools' staffs. Reflective conversations with the teachers following the observations were enlightening. The teachers shared their personal progression from learning about UDL to implementing the Guidelines in their current practice. Interestingly, none of the educators appeared to view themselves as masters of UDL. The MSDE observers had similar reactions to the visits, including pride and excitement about plans to expand the school-wide application of the principles of UDL to support all students.

These classrooms show how far the state has come on its UDL journey. Although this level of implementation is not consistent across Maryland, some schools have already fully implemented UDL. What part has the state played in this journey? How can the state support other schools and districts just embarking on this journey?

HOW THE JOURNEY BEGAN

Maryland's education system consistently ranks as one of the best in the nation, but maintaining the status quo is not enough. Persistent gaps still exist among schools and groups of students. The adoption of the Maryland College and Career Ready Standards emphasized the need to approach instruction differently to achieve the desired outcomes. The state has made closing the achievement gap a priority, and UDL has emerged as a viable framework for providing varied and appropriate support to enable all students to make greater progress.

On May 4, 2010, Maryland became the first state to pass a bill to evaluate the integration of UDL state-wide. The bill, HB 59/SB 467, created the Task Force to Explore the Incorporation of the Principles of Universal Design for Learning into the Education Systems in Maryland. The initial effort was generated by the Maryland Down Syndrome Advocacy Coalition (MDAC), which is part of the National Down Syndrome Society (NDSS). MDAC and NDSS staff first learned about UDL at a conference in September 2008, and the information they received resonated strongly with the organizations' members. After reviewing online resources and attending seminars and workshops on UDL, the MDAC decided to make UDL an organizational priority in Maryland.

MDAC reached out to the MSDE, as well as to parent groups, education leaders, local school boards, the state teachers union, and elected officials. The organization developed a trifold brochure and a website to communicate its message, which they used to bring other stakeholders on board. They built a coalition that spanned general education, special education, and higher education. Working with the MSDE legislative liaison, state legislators, and their aides, MDAC successfully navigated the legislative process to see the bill passed in both the Maryland house and senate, thus paving the way for a state-level UDL task force.

The UDL Task Force

In October 2010, then Governor Martin O'Malley appointed members to the Maryland UDL Task Force. The twenty-two-member task force was composed of a state board of education member, a member of a local school system's board of education, MSDE professionals, a local school system superintendent, university educators, teachers, a representative of the NDSS (who also represented the National UDL Task Force based in Washington, DC), and other educational leaders—some with and some without previous UDL experience. MDSE staff and the UDL Task Force chair planned and coordinated the work of the task force, whose legislative charge was to:

1. Study the effectiveness of UDL as a framework for guiding curriculum design, including goals, teaching methods, instructional materials, and assessments, in order to provide flexibility in the ways information is presented, students respond or demonstrate knowledge and skills, and students are engaged; and reduce barriers in instruction and provide appropriate accommodations, supports, and challenges while maintaining high achievement expectations for all students, including students with disabilities and with limited English proficiency.

2. Study the feasibility of incorporating and applying the principles of UDL into the elementary, secondary, postsecondary, and higher education systems in Maryland with respect to curriculum development; the evaluation and selection of textbooks and other instructional materials; the purchase and use of technology for instructional purposes; teacher preparation and staff development; the development of classroom, district, and statewide assessments, and state grants.

3. Make recommendations related to county education boards incorporating the principles of UDL in the development of local school system policies and procedures.

4. Draft and recommend regulations incorporating the findings of the UDL Task Force.

With just two highly structured face-to-face meetings and some "home-work" in between, the task force explored the foundations of UDL, reviewed the UDL literature, interviewed a variety of UDL experts and stakeholders, and developed tiered recommendations. During the face-to-face meetings, which were held three months apart, the planners were aware of design activities that modeled UDL principles. (See *A Route for Every Learner* [Maryland State Department of Education, 2011] for a complete description of the meeting topics and activities, which could be replicated to support similar efforts in other states. The meeting details provide a procedural recipe for any task force that is considering the effectiveness and feasibility of UDL.)

During the initial meeting, UDL Task Force members formed three sub-committees to address the legislative charge:

- Curriculum, Instruction, and Assessment

- Materials and Technology

- Teacher Preparation and Postsecondary Instruction

Each subcommittee reviewed articles that would help them address their areas of interest, and members were asked to note key ideas, relevance to educational challenges in Maryland, alignment with Maryland's educational initiatives, UDL effectiveness, UDL challenges, and UDL feasibility at all levels of the Maryland education system. Members were also asked to note compelling quotes and real-world examples of UDL in action. To supplement the readings, each subcommittee was asked to identify structured interview questions and conduct phone interviews with targeted policy and research leaders, state and district leaders, university leaders, teachers engaged in UDL implementation, as well as parents and industry leaders.

Between the two main meetings, each of the subcommittees held web-based meetings to track progress, finalize interview questions, and discuss lingering questions and concerns based on the readings. Before the second main meeting, each subcommittee submitted summaries of the selected readings and their phone interviews.

At the final UDL Task Force meeting, the subcommittees made recommendations based on the UDL literature, web resources, and the interviews.

The recommendations were developed at the state, district, school, and classroom levels, and at the postsecondary level. By the end of the second meeting, the UDL Task Force reached a consensus that the UDL principles constitute a commonsense framework for education, and recommended that the principles be incorporated into Maryland's education system. Exit feedback indicated that the meetings and homework assignments proved to be an efficient way to make decisions about the adoption of UDL in Maryland.

"A Route for Every Learner"

The UDL Task Force was expected to produce a written report, but because the members were unpaid volunteers, MSDE provided funds to hire a professional writer to expedite the process and meet the legislative deadline. The seventy-five-page report, "A Route for Every Learner: UDL as a Framework for Supporting Learning and Improving Achievement for All Learners in Maryland, Prekindergarten through Higher Education," summarized the work of the UDL Task Force and its recommendations (Maryland State Department of Education, 2011). A comment period then enabled the task force to garner support from Maryland educators, educational organizations, and parents. The recommendations in the final report, which were sensitive to fiscal constraints, suggested steps Maryland could take to drive the statewide implementation of UDL. The recommendations were developed for the state, district, school, classroom, and higher education levels. The report addressed the following:

- UDL efforts nationwide and in Maryland

- How UDL can improve student outcomes, based on available literature

- Summaries and tables describing the work of the UDL Task Force

- Recommendations for:

  - The Maryland State Board of Education

  - The Maryland State Department of Education

  - Local school systems in Maryland

- Schools and classrooms

- Higher education faculty and teacher education programs

A Grassroots Movement in Local Schools

Although "A Route for Every Learner" was developed at the state level, a grassroots effort continued in many of Maryland's local school systems. This effort began as early as 2009, when UDL began receiving significant national attention as a proactive approach to improving the achievement of all students, including advanced or gifted learners. UDL was originally designed as a support for students with disabilities, but schools and districts recognized quickly that all students would benefit from the flexible environment and variety of instructional strategies UDL offered. As administrators, teachers, and families came to realize that this approach wasn't just for students receiving special education services, a shift in thinking began to occur.

Working across divisions, the UDL message began to move in a more universal direction. The importance of developing a shared understanding and the ability to deliver a consistent message became evident. Exploration of UDL implementation began with cross-departmental conversations about assistive technology, instructional technology, curriculum and instruction, and professional learning, thereby creating a platform for a shared understanding and common message about UDL. Professional learning opportunities were offered in each department and across departments, which built systemic capacity. Each department approached the practice of UDL with a slightly different view, but they came together to form a strong and united front. The orchestration of each faction provided an evolving working model for schools and classrooms. As the central office team started speaking the language of UDL and providing job-embedded coaching, local instructional practices began to change. This strategy created the basis for understanding the UDL principles and practices.

The "soft sell" of UDL and the exploration phase were brought to administrators and instructional staff through practice examples and awareness-based professional learning. The "hard sell" would come at a later date, with strategically planned professional learning opportunities. Support from the central offices helped individual schools to explore and begin the initial implementation phases. Targeted schools and supportive administrators were guided by workshops, ongoing professional learning, and facilitated job-embedded coaching, and change was becoming apparent in select schools. At the same time that some of the local school systems were embracing UDL and working on systemic improvement, work at the state level validated what was being done at the local level. The state's emphasis and strategic work on UDL helped move it from a special education focus to a global vision addressing the instruction of all students.

The tipping point occurred when MSDE convened a statewide leadership meeting, with local school system representatives from general and special education sitting at the same table, hearing a common message, and beginning to plan a collaborative systemic change. From that moment on, the message was clear that, although UDL had been viewed as belonging to special education, in reality the framework could improve instructional practices that include everyone.

Although guided by a common message, the evolving process looked different in each local school system. Some efforts were driven from the administration down to the school level, whereas others were supported by individual teachers and school-based administrators. Parallel worlds were moving in the same direction with a common purpose, as local school systems began to explore UDL and move toward its implementation, and grassroots efforts at the school level were demonstrating UDL in practice and recognizing the need for scaling up. At the state level, advocates and stakeholders heard the message that UDL was a powerful framework that could offer a truly flexible learning environment and "A Route for Every Learner."

The UDL Regulation: COMAR 13A.03.06

Two years after the UDL Task Force was established by the Maryland General Assembly, the Maryland State Board of Education became the first state board to adopt a regulation mandating the application of UDL principles in the curriculum, instructional materials, instruction, professional development, and student assessments. The regulation was COMAR 13A.03.06–Universal Design for Learning.

The regulation was written by a group of MSDE leaders that represented special education and curriculum and instruction. After a review and consultation with local school system superintendents, the regulation was presented to the state board for permission to publish, followed by public comment; it was unanimously adopted in July 2012. As the regulation states, the purpose is to "promote the application of UDL principles to maximize learning opportunities for students, including students with disabilities, students who are gifted and talented, and students who are English language learners, and guide local school systems in the development of curriculum, instructional planning, instructional delivery, material selection, and assessment." The regulation incorporates by reference the UDL Task Force report, "A Route for Every Learner."

Maryland's curriculum is developed at the local school system level; therefore the regulation does not prescribe how each district will implement UDL. However, the regulation did provide a timeline: local school systems were required to develop and revise English language arts and mathematics curriculum in the 2013–2014 school year, using the UDL Guidelines and principles. Beginning in 2014–2015, UDL Guidelines and principles were required in the "development and provision of curriculum, instructional materials, instruction, professional development, and student assessments." School systems were required to select instructional materials that met accessibility requirements and provided multiple options for representation, action and expression, and engagement. Finally, local school system superintendents were required to certify compliance with the regulation in writing to the state superintendent of schools every three years.

The MSDE began to support the implementation of UDL prior to the passage of COMAR 13A.03.06. The statewide professional development initiatives MSDE conducted to support UDL are as follows:

- Maryland education systems

- Principals' Academy

- Governor's Academy

- Gifted and talented educators

- Maryland Co-Teaching Network

- Master Teachers Professional Development

- Education Effectiveness Academies, with follow-up webinars

- Specialized Educators Community of Practice

- College and Career Ready Conference

- State Professional Development Grant

- School Wide Integrated Framework for Transformation

- The Maryland Blackboard Learn site, which hosts UDL resources embedded in lesson plans and unit frameworks to support Maryland College and Career Ready Standards

- Online biology, algebra, government, and English courses as part of Enhancing Teaching and Learning Through the Use of Technology

Professional development around UDL has been provided at a wide variety of general education academies and conferences, and it has been incorporated into grants and other initiatives, including the School Wide Integrated Framework for Transformation (SWIFT).[1] To Maryland's credit, UDL is perceived not as a special education initiative but as a framework to support the learning and achievement of all learners.

To further facilitate UDL implementation in Maryland schools, the state formed the UDL Network, a statewide professional learning community. The UDL Network, which consists of representatives from MSDE, local school districts, and higher education, has planned and supported professional learning opportunities on topics pertinent to UDL. Members of the Maryland UDL Network submitted a draft of a school-level self-assessment rubric to MSDE, which subsequently reviewed and revised the draft, the result being the Local School System Universal Design for Learning Self-Assessment Tool (see Figure 10.1).

---

[1] "SWIFT is a national K–8 technical assistance center that builds school capacity to provide academic and behavioral support to improve outcomes for all students through equity-based inclusion" (see *www.swiftschools.org/*).

Local School System Universal Design for Learning Self-Assessment Tool

COMAR 13A.03.06 Universal Design for Learning (UDL)
Beginning in the 2014-2015 school year, local school systems shall use UDL guidelines and principles, consistent with Regulation .03 of this chapter, in the development and provision of: (1) Curriculum; (2) Instructional materials; (3) Instruction; (4) Professional development; and (5) Student assessments.

The Maryland State Department of Education offers the following continuum to assist local school systems (LSS) in reflecting on the progress of UDL implementation through the application of the Active Implementation Science Frameworks https://unc-fpg-cdi.adobeconnect.com/ai-lesson-quickstart

	Exploratory 1	Installation 2	Initial Implementation 3	Full Implementation 4
	LSS is matching needs, innovation requirements, potential barriers and resources. A UDL Implementation Team is identified.	Necessary resources are acquired or repurposed to support UDL implementation; UDL Implementation Team is operating; sources for training and coaching are identified; initial professional learning has occurred; and organizational supports and protocols are in place.	Practitioners attempt to use newly acquired UDL practices in the classroom with students; coaching and data systems support practitioners; and successful implementation of UDL practices is acknowledged.	UDL is embedded in teaching and learning across all classrooms; practitioners routinely provide UDL opportunities to ensure the success of ALL students; and Implementation Teams ensure the gains in UDL practices are maintained and improved over time.
Please reflect upon the current system-wide status of the implementation of UDL guidelines and principles				

Maryland State Department of Education UDL Implementation Continuum August 2014

FIGURE 10.1 The Local School System Universal Design for Learning Self-Assessment Tool. For the full document, go to *archives.marylandpublicschools. org/.../UDLImplementationContinuumAug2014.doc.* © 2014 MARYLAND STATE DEPARTMENT OF EDUCATION.

The Local School System Universal Design for Learning Self-Assessment Tool is designed to help local Maryland school systems reflect on their progress in implementing UDL by applying the Active Implementation Science Frameworks. School systems rate themselves in the areas of curriculum, instruction, student assessments, and professional learning, according to the following scale:

1. Exploratory

2. Installation

3. Initial Implementation

4. Full Implementation

This tool is more than a checklist; it provides indicators that inform school systems in scaling their implementation, thereby guiding systemic changes in the implementation of the UDL principles. This tool goes beyond the basic principles to focus on specific UDL benchmarks in the curriculum, in instructional materials, in instruction, as part of professional learning, and in student assessments. For example, as a measure of UDL application to the curriculum, local school systems are encouraged to examine the degree to which they provide model lessons or exemplars in all curriculum areas.

Local school systems are also prompted to identify specific objective UDL criteria that guide district and school-level purchasing of both paper and digital or online instructional and assessment materials that support a full range of learner variability and multiple levels of content understanding. All districts are required to report on how they are incorporating UDL into their Bridge to Excellence Master Plans and are encouraged to use the Local School System self-assessment tool to help develop those plans. Each school system also provides a narrative of its successes, challenges, and goals for the full implementation of UDL. These plans, along with the Local School System Universal Design for Learning Self-Assessment Tool, are designed to foster serious reflection and growth. The tools allow MSDE and the school systems to focus on conversations rather than on monitoring, and on technical assistance rather than on accountability.

THE REGULATION IN PRACTICE: CASE STORIES FROM THREE DISTRICTS

One might expect that a state regulatory mandate for the implementation of UDL would guarantee statewide program excellence. However, the certification of compliance that local superintendents are required to make could be seen as a yes/no checklist without evidence of effective implementation. MSDE recognized that, to create an environment that would ensure the successful implementation of UDL statewide, it would need to understand and support UDL practices at the local school system level. Therefore, it held a series of open forums that brought together a diverse group of community and educational stakeholders to engage in meaningful dialogue about the impact UDL has on teaching and learning. Introducing the UDL concept broadly and then bringing it to scale across Maryland also required MSDE to envision how UDL might be implemented in communities, school systems, and schools and classrooms.

One successful strategy for bringing UDL to scale is to identify districts that are committed to operationalizing the UDL framework. This integration of UDL looks different in each school district. In the following sections, we spotlight three Maryland districts that are implementing UDL using very different methods. Montgomery County Public Schools (MCPS) uses an application process to select schools and staff willing to commit to the systematic implementation of UDL, Allegany County Public Schools began by piloting the use of the UDL framework in a middle and high school, and Queen Anne's County systematically connected UDL implementation with its 1:1 laptop initiative. Examining these UDL implementation efforts is a reminder that Maryland's school districts are as varied as its learners.

Montgomery County

MCPS is a large suburban school district bordering on Washington, DC. Initial UDL implementation efforts at MCPS were concentrated in the targeted schools, starting with two and scaling up to twenty-four over the course of five years. Some of the schools brought selected staff members together in small professional learning communities (PLCs), and then used these staff members as part of the UDL leadership teams that were focused on expanding UDL in each school. The initial stage of implementation consisted of instructional procedures and strategies for teaching and learning using the UDL principles and Guidelines, which were incorporated into professional development workshops.

In 2009, UDL implementation was initiated in one elementary and one middle school. The level shifted from "paper implementation" to "process implementation," which included staff training, classroom supervision, and reporting on data to the school principals. Although there were ample resources at that time to explain UDL, few resources existed to guide its implementation. Over time, classroom observation tools and survey instruments were developed to measure the fidelity of UDL practices and, thus, the shift to "performance" after "process" implementation began.

As a first step in the school-based implementation of UDL, it was critical to identify staff members who were well versed in UDL to coordinate integration efforts. Initially, members of the district's High Incidence Accessible Technology (HIAT) team served as part-time UDL consultants, sharing ideas and strategies and delivering professional development to the two schools. HIAT members spent at least one day per week at each school and met bimonthly with the UDL leadership teams that had been established at each school. As the number of schools engaged in UDL implementation increased, the role of the UDL consultants became more apparent. Having one full-time UDL consultant for every six schools implementing UDL was considered optimal.

The UDL consultants were tasked with the following:

- Coordinate efforts with central administration

- Assist in the selection of schools

- Meet with principals to clarify expectations

- Provide schools with basic information on UDL

- Provide training and coaching to school-based UDL facilitators

- Provide training on what it means to be part of a developing PLC

- Train UDL leadership teams on the UDL principles and Guidelines

- Support the ongoing development of the PLCs

- Provide on-site support and conduct UDL walkthroughs

- Track data, examine trends, troubleshoot, problem solve, and unravel misconceptions about UDL

The following is a timeline of events that helped schools in MCPS get ready to begin the UDL integration phase at the onset of the school year.

January/February:

- Initiate the school application process.

- Meet with principals.

- Meet with central administration to select participating schools.

March/April:

- Present information about UDL to each participating school.

- Initiate the staff application process.

May/June:

- Meet with principals to select members of the UDL Leadership Team for each school.

- Meet with the on-site UDL facilitator and the UDL Leadership Team to provide information and expectations for the year to come.

July/August:

- Provide professional learning opportunities on the foundations of UDL.

September to April:

- All first-year UDL Leadership Teams participate in a three-credit, online forum that serves to foster the development of a UDL professional learning community.

Schools were selected using an online application process. An administrator in the central office sent memoranda to school principals that briefly described the opportunity and invited them to apply. Links to the online application and to video testimonials from principals who had participated in previous years were provided. A document file was attached that described the UDL implementation project in detail and explained the goals and expectations, the benefits and deliverables, timelines, the administrative commitment, the purpose of the PLC, the staff selection process, and expectations.

Face-to-face information sessions were also scheduled to provide information and answer questions about the UDL projects.

The online application served multiple purposes. It reinforced the level of commitment required and provided information on the technology tools available in classrooms. The application also allowed the evaluators who were selecting the schools to gauge whether the UDL implementation project would complement or compete with other priority initiatives.

This approach was adopted based on the recognition that principals must have a clear understanding up front of what is needed to develop an effective PLC. For example, educators need time in the master schedule to plan collaboratively with UDL in mind, and both principals and staff need to understand the importance of measuring the fidelity of implementation.

At the end of the application period, central office administrators met with the UDL consultants to select the schools that would participate, after which they met with the selected schools' principals. In these informal discussions, the administrators clarified the scope and sequence of the project, and gave examples of the effectiveness of UDL in neighboring schools. They also clarified that, in the first half of the school year, the UDL leadership team would be focused on implementing UDL in their classrooms with increasing fidelity. Outreach to the rest of the school staff would take place in the second half of the school year.

Members of the school-based UDL leadership teams were also selected by application. Full school meetings were held to introduce the UDL projects, answer questions, and encourage staff members to apply, after which the staff received an email with a link to an online application and a document that described the project in detail. Once the UDL leadership team was selected, they met with the UDL consultant to outline goals and expectations and answer questions.

Learning management system software provided ongoing information relative to UDL, gave the participants the opportunity to reflect and share ideas related to UDL, and enabled the PLC members to develop a professional network across the participating schools. It was important for the staff to understand that this online environment was much more than a course or a series of lessons, that it was a forum for building a PLC that enabled staff to reflect on educational practices by sharing stories that informed practice. It was also a vehicle for gaining the confidence to explore new ways of teaching and to collaboratively build an understanding of what UDL looks like in the classroom.

It was essential that staff participation was truly voluntary. School administrators and the UDL consultant reviewed the staff applications collaboratively, selecting eight to twelve people from each discipline who were from no more than eight classrooms per school. For example, general education teachers, special educators, media specialists, and paraprofessionals were encouraged to apply, and those chosen were clearly motivated to try new teaching methods and materials, and wanted to learn more about UDL and technology integration.

We next highlight Allegany County's journey through the preparation phase of UDL implementation. We describe the processes that ensured that this large suburban school district was ready to start the UDL integration phase across multiple schools. Reaching full-scale UDL integration has its challenges, which can be minimized by having a clear and systematic preparation process from the outset. The advantage of building UDL from within a school culture is that the process can marshal the energies and enthusiasm of teacher leaders, who then spread the message to their peers. Fixsen, Naoom, Blase, Friedman, and Wallace (2005) suggest that school-wide implementation efforts are not as productive as integrating the UDL process slowly and systematically. However, bringing UDL to scale in four or five schools at one time is not efficient in a large district like MCPS, as it would take more than forty years. The goal, therefore, was not to adopt UDL one school at a time but to approach the implementation process in a way that enabled UDL to gain a firm foothold in educational practices and concretely demonstrate the benefits to the school district as a whole.

Allegany County

During the 2015–2016 school year, Allegany County Public Schools (ACPS), located in the northwest part of Maryland, successfully piloted the integration of two instructional frameworks: Gradual Release of Responsibility (GRR) and Universal Design for Learning.

Phases of the Lesson Study Model of Professional Learning

Phases were used with the ACPS pilot cohorts; they are also being used during the 2016–2017 school year:

Phase 1:

Secondary science and social studies teachers will work in their respective cohorts to establish short-term and long-term goals specific to the MDCCRS, and the GRR and UDL instructional frameworks that will lead to achievement of twenty-first-century skills for all students.

Phase 2:

Using the Lesson Study Model, secondary science and social studies teachers will build upon three previously taught lessons in the effort to align the Gradual Release of Responsibility instructional framework with the principles, Guidelines, and checkpoints of Universal Design for Learning as they plan research lessons.

Phase 3:

While one teacher facilitates the learning of the planned lesson, the other teachers and a "knowledgeable observer" will observe the learning with a specific focus on whether the needs of all students have been met during all components of the lesson via eliminating potential learning barriers.

Phase 4:

Teachers and the knowledgeable observer will analyze the data collected during each of the three lessons in the effort to determine what worked in the lesson and what did not work in the lesson with a specific focus on whether the needs of all students were met during all components of the lesson or if learning barriers still existed within the lessons and what could be done to eliminate such learning barriers.

Professional development in ACPS was focused on the Japanese Lesson Study model (Doig & Groves, 2011), along with the UDL principles, Guidelines, and checkpoints. The district's integration of both frameworks was based on the book *Better Learning Through Structured Teaching: A Framework for the Gradual Release of Responsibility* (Fisher & Frey, 2014), as well as publications from CAST. Both frameworks gave students engaging and rigorous barrier-free learning environments that prepared them for post–high school life. Because of the pilot's success, ACPS decided to integrate both frameworks into science and social studies classes in grades 6–12 during the 2016–2017 school year. This integration of GRR and UDL was supported by the literature:

> There is room and merit in marrying existing scientifically valid practice with innovation supported under the UDL framework. However, explicit instructional design and practice, grounded in strong theory and reliable and valid measurement, is needed to help ensure that specially designed instruction and UDL's relationship is extended and bolstered on the basis of evidence for students with LD. As long as these standards are met, teachers can, and should consider UDL as a guiding framework that may interface with existing and relevant instructional approaches. (Kennedy, Newman, Meyer, Alves, & Lloyd, 2014, p. 72)

Meo (2008) adds that "UDL emphasizes teachers as coaches or guides, learning as a process, and cooperative learning. In these approaches, teachers support learning rather than impart knowledge, and students construct knowledge rather than passively receive it" (p. 23). Although the author refers specifically to UDL, this notion also aligns well with the GRR, and the simultaneous integration of GRR and UDL helped to eliminate "confusion about what UDL is, how it relates to other initiatives, and how to implement it" (Kennedy et al., 2014, p. 72).

After this approach was piloted during the second semester of the 2015–2016 school year, many participants responded favorably to the work. Here are a few of their responses:

> *Question:* How do the principles and Guidelines of UDL align with the GRR instructional framework?

Answer: "The principles of UDL go hand-in-hand with the Gradual Release of Responsibility Instructional Framework: providing students multiple means of representation during Focused and Guided Instruction helps all students to build skills and understanding; providing multiple means of action and expression during Collaborative and Independent Learning helps all students to practice and apply skills and understanding without barriers, and providing multiple means of engagement supports all students through each of the four components of the GRR Framework."—Cohort Reflection (2016)

Question: As a result of your UDL Leadership Project experience, are you more cognizant of meeting the needs of *all* students as you prepare and carry out lessons?

Answer: "Yes, I am more cognizant of meeting the needs of all students. I am excited about making lessons more accessible and engaging and about assessing learning in ways that allow students to utilize their strengths."
—Participant Reflection (2016)

During the 2015–2016 school year, twelve cohorts of secondary science and social studies teachers used the collaborative Japanese Lesson Study model of professional learning to integrate GRR and UDL into their lesson plans. Once again, the literature supports the Japanese Lesson Study model in the implementation of UDL principles, Guidelines, and checkpoints. Throughout the Planning for All Learners (PAL) process, each team member draws from his or her educational expertise and experiences to design a curriculum that ensures that all learners gain knowledge, skills, and enthusiasm for learning. Collaboration is a key ingredient among the team members, with all focusing on developing a flexible curriculum that supports all learners' achievement of identified goals (Meo, 2008, p. 23).

After the ACPS pilot study, participants responded to survey questions related to use of the Japanese Lesson Study model. Here are a few of the questions and responses:

Question: Was it valuable to integrate the expectations of the GRR and UDL while utilizing the Lesson Study Model?

Answer: "The Lesson Study Model is beneficial to teachers. It offers an opportunity for collaboration and shared creativity. It allows us to draw on the strengths of each team member in designing lessons that include activities or

resources that we otherwise would not be comfortable creating or using....
The use of GRR and UDL provides more opportunities for students to learn
the material, to be engaged, and to ultimately feel successful in the classroom
setting. It allows the students to be stakeholders in the education process
because they are given the opportunity to have input into the process with a
multitude of choices for what best suits them."—Cohort Reflection (2016)

Answer: "Absolutely. Using something new as a team makes it less threatening.
The ability to ask each other questions about how they interpreted the different parts of GRR was helpful.... Adding UDL was an enlightening experience
to see the choices the students picked as they worked their way through the
various stations. Adding UDL was easier than expected with the help of the
other teachers."—Cohort Reflection (2016)

As noted by Doig and Groves (2011), the Japanese Lesson Study model
of professional learning has the potential to lead to sustainability because it
gives teachers "ownership" over their professional learning, it leads to consistent "collaboration" among colleagues, and it "enables teachers to build on
their efforts and refine their understandings" (pp. 90–91).

If students are to be prepared upon high school graduation to face the
demands of the twenty-first century, educator-centered classrooms across the
nation need to be replaced by student-centered classrooms, in which educators do not deconstruct "complex real-life phenomena into little parts" and do
not depend on tests that "are linear, sequential, and time restricted" (Scheer,
Noweski, & Meinel, 2012, p. 10). John Dewey, the early twentieth-century
education reformer, claimed that educators need to provide "construction
through instruction" (Scheer et al., 2012, p. 10). Careful and intentional cycli-
cal planning using the Japanese Lesson Study model and integration of the
GRR and UDL instructional frameworks can empower teachers to "design
learning experiences" (p. 10) that will help prepare students for post–high
school life. Integration of the two instructional frameworks also creates a
"good learning design" that ultimately allows students to construct their own
knowledge as the teacher/facilitator "enables" them to do so (p. 10). This is
the path ACPS has chosen as it strives for great teaching and great learning
for every student every day.

Queen Anne's County

Located on the picturesque eastern shore of Maryland, Queen Anne's County Public Schools (QACPS) has embarked on a digital transformation highlighted by a 1:1 device program for all students, which involved the integration of Chromebooks in grades 3–8 and laptops in grades 9–12. The effort, which was initially met with both excitement and apprehension, has resulted in transformative teaching practices. QACPS students are now collaborating via Google Apps, accessing online textbooks, and conducting virtual experiments. Nevertheless, the implementation of these devices has raised important questions, including where UDL fits within this new 1:1 environment, and whether students are getting "flexible options" if so much work is now done on a device. During the 2015–2016 school year, QACPS tackled these issues with a three-pronged approach focused on curriculum, instructional materials, and professional development.

Queen Anne's County began by hiring a consultant to conduct a comprehensive curriculum audit. One component of the audit was identifying UDL practices in curriculum documents, such as lesson plans. The results of the audit are now driving the creation of a county-wide curriculum guide that highlights blended instruction while simultaneously embedding UDL principles. To ensure that UDL is consistently implemented during the planning stage, QACPS has specifically identified UDL in all lesson-planning templates. Moreover, to ensure the fidelity of UDL practices, teacher specialists have created an electronic walkthrough tool in Google Forms that building leaders can use as they conduct instructional rounds. This enables teachers to receive feedback on the UDL practices (both instructional and environmental) employed in their classrooms. Central office staff will use this data to evaluate how UDL practices are being integrated in teaching and learning throughout the county. They are focused specifically on the 1:1 program providing flexible options for all students to ensure that they have a "choice and voice."

The second phase of the QACPS effort is focused on instructional materials. In the past, instructional materials often were purchased at the school level, which led to some disparity among schools and classrooms. To identify areas of need, the district's facilitator of digital teaching and learning conducted individual walkthroughs of all classrooms, taking note of three primary concerns: (1) flexible options in the classroom environment, (2) equitable instructional materials, and (3) teacher training needs. The data gathered from these informative visits were combined with a system-wide instructional budget review, after which it was determined that purchasing software, including interventions, should be done through the central office to ensure that all students have access to digitally rich curriculum they can view on their devices or have projected in the classroom.

During these classroom walkthroughs, the UDL principle of representation, specifically as it relates to providing options for perception, emerged as a major obstacle. Some schools were able to project materials on large interactive whiteboards, whereas others were still relying on antiquated televisions mounted high in the classrooms. Students in those classrooms were not able to see and interact with the digital curriculum. As a result, the district made it a priority for the 2016–2017 academic year to equip every classroom with an interactive whiteboard display to ensure that all students can access the digital curriculum in a whole-group setting.

Web 2.0 tools have made available a plethora of websites and programs that teachers are using in their instruction. However, classroom visits also revealed that teachers are overwhelmed by the sheer volume of resources available and are frustrated because of the limitations embedded in much of the free software (e.g., the ability to make only a fifteen-second video). QACPS has committed to purchasing district-wide software to ensure that all teachers and students have tools that enable them to author work in various formats, present information in multiple ways, and stay engaged in the learning process.

The last piece of the UDL puzzle for QACPS centered on how best to deliver professional development. In the past, teachers have attended UDL courses after school, schools have presented UDL strategies at their faculty meetings, and teachers have gone on UDL scavenger hunts to identify examples of UDL in the learning environment. During the 2015–2016 school year, QACPS took a different approach by creating a bi-monthly newsletter that has highlighted different tools for engagement, representation, and expression. Titled *Inspiring Innovation,* the newsletter features a section called "Tech Tools Through the UDL Lens" that has given teachers an informal opportunity to deepen their understanding of how UDL tools fit within the new 1:1 system. Finally, QACPS approached all technology training by joining UDL with the substitution, augmentation, modification, redefinition (SAMR) model, which is a framework for how technology impacts teaching and learning. Teachers are immersed in providing flexible options for their students by working up the SAMR ladder to ensure that they are using technology as a way to redefine learning experiences.

QACPS is convinced that introducing digital devices has allowed students to access information differently (representation), to create information differently (expression), and to share information with a worldwide digital audience (engagement). The 1:1 program at QACPS is not viewed simply as a technology revolution but as an information revolution. By focusing the digital transformation on the powerful flow of information instead of on the device, QACPS has been able to integrate UDL effectively into everyday instructional practice.

THE PATH FORWARD

As Maryland continues to implement UDL in its school systems, the MSDE and its school systems and higher education partners are committed to providing professional learning that is customized for schools and educators who are at different stages along the implementation continuum. The state recognizes the variability among districts and schools, and offers options and support during each phase of UDL implementation: exploration, preparation, integration, scaling, and optimization. It is equally important that districts find opportunities to communicate, to share best practices, and to learn from each other as they move forward. MSDE is committed to sustaining and expanding the UDL network to promote collaboration across local school systems and their higher education partners.

Parallel to the state UDL initiatives at the district level, Maryland's higher education institutions have also begun to implement UDL more systematically. UDL principles have been embedded into general and special education instruction at Johns Hopkins University, Towson University, and Goucher College, and McDaniel College sponsors an annual conference that focuses on classroom implementation of UDL. Two additional districts have collaborated with Towson University to sponsor summer institutes, which has created opportunities for presenters from Maryland's institutions of higher education and its local school districts.

The route Maryland has traveled to arrive at its current stage of UDL implementation is a model for all states. Maryland's recognition of UDL through investigation, task force efforts, and the resultant report, "A Route for Every Learner," led to a state regulation that has helped to move Maryland from UDL awareness to implementation. Much progress has occurred as the state moves forward with UDL integration in keeping with COMAR regulations. At the local school level, implementation continues to grow and scale upward. The Maryland State Department of Education remains committed to facilitating cross-departmental awareness and implementation of UDL. To maintain this trajectory of growth and sustainability, the MSDE continues to provide both universal and targeted technical assistance to all local school systems. Consistently ranked by *Education Week* as among the best public school systems in the nation, the MSDE leads the way in philosophy, in pedagogy, and in practice, and it recognizes that the continued application of UDL in all learning environments is a framework that meets the challenge and the promise of learner variability.

References

PREFACE

Meyer, A., Rose, D. H., & Gordon, D. (2014). *Universal Design for Learning: Theory and practice*. Wakefield, MA: CAST Professional Publishing.

Rappolt-Schlichtmann, G., Daley, S. G., & Rose, L. T. (Eds.). (2012). *A research reader in Universal Design for Learning*. Cambridge, MA: Harvard Education Press.

Rose, D. H., & Meyer, A. (2002). *Teaching every student in the digital age: Universal Design for Learning*. Alexandria, VA: ASCD.

Rose, D. H., & Meyer, A. (Eds.). (2006). *A practical reader in Universal Design for Learning*. Cambridge, MA: Harvard Education Press.

Rose, D. H., Meyer, A., & Hitchcock, C. (2005). *The universally designed classroom: Accessible curriculum and digital technologies*. Cambridge, MA: Harvard Education Press.

CHAPTER 1

CAST. (2012). *UDL strategy guide*. Wakefield, MA: Author.

Code of Maryland Regulations (COMAR). 13A.03.06 (2012).

Dole, J., & Sinatra, G. (1998). Reconceptualizing change in the cognitive construction of knowledge. *Educational Psychologist, 33*(2/3), 109–128.

Every Student Succeeds Act of 2015. U.S.C 114-95 § 114 (2015).

Fixsen, D. L., Naoom, S. F., Blase, K. A., Friedman, R. M., & Wallace, F. (2005). *Implementation research: A synthesis of the literature* (FMHI Publication #231). Retrieved from *http://ctndisseminationlibrary.org/PDF/nirnmonograph.pdf.*

Higher Education Opportunity Act. 20 U.S.C. § 110-315 (2008).

Meyer, A., Rose, D. H., & Gordon, D. (2014). *Universal Design for Learning: Theory and practice.* Wakefield, MA: CAST Professional Publishing.

Nelson, L. L., Arthur, E. J., Jensen, W. R., & Van Horn, G. (2011, April). Trading textbooks for technology: New opportunities for learning. *Phi Delta Kappan, 92*(7), 46–50.

Partnership for 21st Century Learning. (2009). *Framework for 21st century learning.* Retrieved from *www.p21.org/about-us/p21-framework.*

Pintrich, P. R., Marx, R. P., & Boyle, R. A. (1993). Beyond cold conceptual change: The role of motivational beliefs and classroom contextual factors in the process of conceptual change. *Review of Educational Research, 63*(2), 167–200.

Posner, G., Strike, K., Hewson, P., & Gertzog, W. (1982). Accommodation of a scientific conception: Towards a theory of conceptual change. *Science Education, 67,* 489–508. Retrieved from *http://onlinelibrary.wiley.com/journal/10.1002/(ISSN)1098-237X.*

Rappolt-Schlichtmann, G., Daley, S. G., & Rose, L. T. (Eds.). (2012). *A research reader in Universal Design for Learning.* Cambridge, MA: Harvard Education Press.

Rose, D. H., & Meyer, A. (2002). *Teaching every student in the digital age: Universal Design for Learning.* Alexandria, VA: ASCD.

Sadera, W., & Hargrave, C. (2005). Conceptual change in preservice teacher preparation. In C. Vrasidas & G. V. Glass (Eds.), *Preparing teachers to teach with technology* (pp. 291–302). Greenwich, CT: Information Age.

Tillema, H. H., & Knol, W. E. (1997). Promoting student teacher learning through conceptual change or direct instruction. *Teacher and Teacher Education, 13,* 579–595.

U.S. Department of Education, Office of Educational Technology. (2010). *National education technology plan.* Retrieved from *https://www.ed.gov/sites/default/files/netp2010.pdf.*

U.S. Department of Education, Office of Educational Technology. (2016). *National education technology plan.* Retrieved from *http://tech.ed.gov/netp/.*

CHAPTER 2

Berquist, E., & Sadera, W. (2015). An examination of teachers' and administrators' conceptions about UDL: Considerations for applying conceptual change based professional development. In E. Gardener (Ed.), *Implementing Universal Design for Learning: Selected papers from the 2014 UDL-IRN summit.* Lawrence, KS: The Universal Design for Learning Implementation and Research Network.

CAST. (2010). *UDL pedagogical considerations.* Wakefield, MA: Author.

CAST. (2011). *About UDL.* Wakefield, MA: Author.

CAST. (2012). *UDL strategy guide.* Wakefield, MA: Author.

CAST. (2014). *UDL Guidelines graphic organizer.* Wakefield, MA: Author.

Darling-Hammond, L., & McLaughlin, M. W. (2011). Policies that support professional development in an era of reform. *Phi Delta Kappan, 92*(6), 81–92.

Hall, T., Rose, D., & Meyer, A. (Eds.). (2012). *Universal Design for Learning: Practical applications.* Cambridge, MA: Harvard Education Press.

Higher Education Opportunity Act. 20 U.S.C. § 110-315 (2008).

Posner, G., Strike, K., Hewson. P., & Gertzog, W. (1982). Accommodation of a scientific conception: Towards a theory of conceptual change. *Science Education, 67,* 489–508.

Rose, D. H., & Meyer, A. (2002). *Teaching every student in the digital age: Universal Design for Learning.* Alexandria, VA: ASCD.

Sadera, W., & Hargrave, C. (2005). Conceptual change in preservice teacher preparation. In C. Vrasidas & G. V. Glass (Eds.), *Preparing teachers to teach with technology* (pp. 291–302). Greenwich, CT: Information Age.

Tillema, H. (1997). Promoting conceptual change in learning to teach. *Asia-Pacific Journal of Teacher Education, 25*(1), 7. Retrieved from *http://atea.edu.au/index.php?option=com_content&task=view&id=16&Itemid=17*.

U.S. Department of Education, Office of Educational Technology. (2010). *National education technology plan*. Retrieved from *https://www.ed.gov/sites/default/files/netp2010.pdf*.

U.S. Department of Education, Office of Educational Technology. (2016). *National education technology plan*. Retrieved from *http://tech.ed.gov/netp/*.

Varela, A. (2012). Three major sins of professional development: How can we make it better? *Education Digest, 78*(4), 17. Retrieved from *www.eddigest.com*.

Wei, R. C., Darling-Hammond, L., Andree, A., Richardson, N., & Orphanos, S. (2009). *Professional learning in the learning profession: A status report on teacher development in the United States and abroad*. Dallas, TX: National Staff Development Council.

CHAPTER 3

Augmented reality. (n.d.). *Wikipedia*. Retrieved from *https://en.wikipedia.org/wiki/Augmented_reality*.

Briggs, B. (2016). *Keep the quote*. [Blog post] Retrieved from *https://miss-5th.blogspot.com/2016/06/keep-quote.html?m=1*.

Gagné, R. M. (1965). *The conditions of learning*. New York: Holt, Rinehart, & Winston.

Gagné, R. M., Briggs, L. J., & Wager, W. W. (1992). *Principles of instructional design* (4th ed.). Ft. Worth, TX: Harcourt Brace Jovanovich.

Horn, M. B., Staker, H., & Christensen, C. M. (2015). *Blended: Using disruptive innovation to improve schools.* San Francisco, CA: Jossey-Bass.

Khadjooi, K., Rostami, K., & Ishaq, S. (2011). How to use Gagné's model of instructional design in teaching psychomotor skills. *Gastroenterology & Hepatology from Bed to Bench, 4*(3), 116–119.

Merrill, M. D., Drake, L., Lacy, M. J., & Pratt, J. (1996). Reclaiming instructional design. *Educational Technology,* 36(5), 5–7. Retrieved from *http://mdavidmerrill.com/Papers/Reclaiming.pdf.*

Meyer, A., Rose, D. H., & Gordon, D. (2014). *Universal Design for Learning: Theory and practice.* Wakefield, MA: CAST Professional Publishing.

Muhtaris, K., & Ziemke, K. (2015). *Amplify: Digital teaching and learning in the K-6 classroom.* Portsmouth, NH: Heinemann.

National Center on Universal Design for Learning. (2012). *UDL implementation: A process of change.* Online UDL Series, No. 3. Retrieved from *http://udlseries.udlcenter.org/presentations/udl_implementation.html.*

Rappolt-Schlichtmann, G., Daley, S. G., & Rose, L. T. (2012). *A research reader in Universal Design for Learning.* Cambridge, MA: Harvard Education Press.

Ray, K., Laufenberg, D., & Bejerede, M. (2016). *Guide to choosing digital content and curriculum.* Retrieved from *www.centerdigitaled.com/paper/Guide-to-Choosing-Digital-Content-and-Curriculum-41458.html.*

Wolpert-Gawron, H. (2015). *Kids speak out on student engagement.* Retrieved from *www.edutopia.org/blog/student-engagement-stories-heather-wolpert-gawron.*

CHAPTER 4

City, E. A., Elmore, R. F., Fiarman, S. E., & Teitel, L. (2009). *Instructional rounds in education: A network approach to improving learning and teaching.* Cambridge, MA: Harvard Education Press.

Covey, S. (2014). *The 7 habits of highly effective people: Powerful lessons in change.* New York: Free Press.

DuFour, R., DuFour, R., Eaker, R., & Many, T. (2006). *Learning by doing.* Bloomington, IN: Solution Tree.

Meyer, A., Rose, D. H., & Gordon, D. (2014). *Universal Design for Learning: Theory and practice.* Wakefield, MA: CAST Professional Publishing.

Muhtaris, K., & Ziemke, K. (2015). *Amplify: Digital teaching and learning in the K-6 classroom.* Portsmouth, NH: Heinemann.

Novak, K. (2014). *UDL now! A teacher's Monday-morning guide to implementing Common Core Standards using Universal Design for Learning.* Wakefield, MA: CAST Professional Publishing.

Waller, W. (2014). *The sociology of teaching.* Eastford, CT: Martino Fine Books.

CHAPTER 5

CAST. (2012a). *A tale of four districts.* Wakefield, MA: Author. Retrieved from *www.udlcenter.org/implementation/fourdistricts.*

CAST. (2012b). *UDL implementation strategy guide.* Wakefield, MA: Author.

CAST. (2012c). *Crosswalk between Universal Design for Learning and the Danielson Framework for Teaching.* Wakefield, MA: Author. Retrieved from *www.udlcenter.org/implementation/udl-danielson-crosswalk.*

Meyer, A., Rose, D. H., & Gordon, D. (2014). *Universal Design for Learning: Theory and practice.* Wakefield, MA: CAST Professional Publishing.

Novak, K. (2014). *UDL now! A teacher's Monday-morning guide to implementing Common Core Standards using Universal Design for Learning.* Wakefield, MA: CAST Professional Publishing.

CHAPTER 6

CAST. (2012). *A tale of four districts.* Wakefield, MA: Author. Retrieved from *www.udlcenter.org/implementation/fourdistricts.*

Fixsen, D. L., Naoom, S. F., Blase, K. A., Friedman, R. M., & Wallace, F. (2005). Implementation research: A synthesis of the literature. Tampa: University of South Florida, Louis de la Parte Florida Mental Health Institute, NIRN (FMHI Publication #231).

Katz, J., & Sugden, R. (2013). The three-block model of universal design for learning implementation in a high school. *Canadian Journal of Educational Administration & Policy, 141,* 1–28.

Kraglund-Gauthier, W. L., Young, D. C., & Kell, E. (2014). Teaching students with disabilities in post-secondary landscapes: Navigating elements of inclusion, differentiation, universal design for learning, and technology. *Transformative Dialogues: Teaching & Learning Journal, 7*(3), 1–9.

Lopes-Murphy, S. (2012). Universal design for learning: Preparing secondary education teachers in training to increase academic accessibility of high school English learners. *Clearing House, 85,* 226–230. doi:10.1080/00098 655.2012.693549.

National Center on Universal Design for Learning. (2012). *UDL implementation: A process of change.* Online UDL Series, No. 3. Retrieved from *http:// udlseries.udlcenter.org/presentations/udl_implementation.html.*

Meyer, A., Rose, D. H., & Gordon, D. (2014). *Universal Design for Learning: Theory and practice.* Wakefield, MA: CAST Professional Publishing.

Novak, K. (2014). *UDL now! A teacher's Monday-morning guide to implementing Common Core Standards using Universal Design for Learning.* Wakefield, MA: CAST Professional Publishing.

Tzivinikou, S. (2014). Universal design for learning—Application in higher education: A Greek paradigm. *Problems of Education in the 21st Century, 60,* 156–166.

CHAPTER 7

Friend M., & Cook, L. (2012). *Interactions: Collaboration skills for school professionals* (7th ed.) New York: Pearson.

Green, John. (2012). *The fault in our stars.* Dutton Books: New York.

Hall, T. E., Meyer, A., & Rose, D. H. (2012). *Universal Design for Learning in the classroom: Practical applications.* New York: Guilford Press.

Meyer, A., Rose, D. H., & Gordon, D. (2014). *Universal Design for Learning: Theory and practice.* Wakefield, MA: CAST Professional Publishing.

Murawski, W. W., & Lochner, W. W. (2010). Observing co-teaching: What to ask for, look for, and listen for. *Intervention in School and Clinic, 46,* 174–183. doi: 10.1177/1053451210378165.

National Center on Universal Design for Learning. (2014). *UDL Guidelines—Version 2.0.* Retrieved from *www.udlcenter.org/aboutudl/udlguidelines.*

Ralabate, P. K. (2016). *Your UDL lesson planner: The step-by-step guide for teaching all learners.* Baltimore, MD: Brookes Publishing.

CHAPTER 8

Ambrose, D. (1987). *Managing complex change.* Pittsburgh, PA: The Enterprise Ltd.

National Center on Universal Design for Learning. (2012). *UDL implementation: A process of change.* Online UDL Series, No. 3. Retrieved from *http://udlseries.udlcenter.org/presentations/udl_implementation.html.*

Rose, D. H., & Meyer, A. (2002). *Teaching every student in the digital age: Universal Design for Learning.* Alexandria, VA: ASCD.

U.S. Department of Education, Office of Special Education Programs. (2017). National Technical Assistance Center on Positive Behavioral Interventions and Supports. Retrieved from *www.pbis.org.*

CHAPTER 9

Al-Azawei, A., Serenelli, F., & Lundqvist, K. (2016). Universal Design for Learning (UDL): A content analysis of peer-reviewed journal papers from 2012 to 2015. *Journal of the Scholarship of Teaching & Learning, 16*(3), 39–56. doi:10.14434/josotl.v16i3.19295.

CAST. (2011). *Universal Design for Learning guidelines, version 2.0.* Wakefield, MA: National Center on Universal Design for Learning.

Chita-Tegmark, M., Gravel, J. W., Serpa, M. B., Domings, Y., & Rose, D. H. (2012). Using the Universal Design for Learning framework to support culturally diverse learners. *Journal of Education, 192*(1), 17–22.

Code of Maryland Regulations (COMAR) 13A.03.06 (2012).

Pace, D., & Blue, E. (2010). Cutting edge educators: Preservice teachers' use of technology within universal design for learning framework. *Insights on Learning Disabilities, 7*(2), 19–29. Retrieved from *www.ldworldwide.org/educators/ild-educators.*

Rose, D. H., & Meyer, A. (2002). *Teaching every student in the digital age: Universal Design for Learning.* Alexandria, VA: ASCD.

CHAPTER 10

Code of Maryland Regulations (COMAR) 13A.03.06 (2012).

Doig, B., & Groves, S. (2011). Japanese lesson study: Teachers professional development through communities of inquiry. *Mathematics Teacher Education and Development, 13*(1), 77–93.

Fisher, D., & Frey, N. (2014). *Better learning through structured teaching: A framework for the gradual release of responsibility.* Alexandria, VA: ASCD.

Fixsen, D. L., Naoom, S. F., Blase, K. A., Friedman, R. M., & Wallace, F. (2005). *Implementation research: A synthesis of the literature.* Tampa: University of

South Florida, Louis de la Parte Florida Mental Health Institute, National Implementation Research Network.

Kennedy, M. J., Newman T. C., Meyer, J. P., Alves, K., & Lloyd, J. (2014). Using evidence-based multimedia to improve vocabulary performance of adolescents with LD. *Learning Disability Quarterly, 37*(2), 71–86. doi: 10.1177/0731948713507262.

Maryland State Department of Education. (2011). *A route for every learner: Universal Design for Learning as a framework for supporting and improving achievement for all learners in Maryland, prekindergarten through higher education.* Baltimore, MD: Author.

Meo, G. (2008). Curriculum planning for ALL learners: Applying Universal Design for Learning (UDL) to a high school reading comprehension program. *Preventing School Failure, 52*(2), 21–30. doi:10.3200/PSFL.52.2.21-30.

Scheer, A., Noweski, C., & Meinel, C. (2012). Transforming constructivist learning into action: Design thinking in education. *Design and Technology Education, 17*(3), 8–19.

About the Authors

Elizabeth Berquist, EdD, is an assistant professor in the Department of Special Education at Towson University in Towson, Maryland. She works with preservice and in-service educators and teaches a variety of undergraduate and graduate courses. Prior to joining the Towson faculty, Dr. Berquist was employed by the Baltimore County Public School system as a middle school and high school social studies educator, special educator, and central office curriculum and instruction staff member. Dr. Berquist has served as a consultant for the Maryland State Department of Education (MDSE) and is a member of the CAST UDL faculty cadre. She has worked on the implementation of Universal Design for Learning (UDL) with school districts and institutes of higher education across the United States and was a facilitator for the Bill & Melinda Gates Foundation UDL implementation project. She is a frequent presenter at national conferences and an invited facilitator for the Harvard Graduate School of Education UDL Institute. She is featured in the UDL Series Implementation video produced by the National Center on Universal Design for Learning. Most recently, Dr. Berquist founded "All In, " a group dedicated to empowering educators, family members, and community leaders with the skills and dispositions necessary to support and celebrate learner variability. Dr. Berquist holds certifications in social studies, special education, and administration. She received a BA in American studies and history from Washington College, a master's degree in special education from Towson University, a certificate in administration and supervision from Goucher College, and a doctoral degree in instructional technology from Towson University.

George D. Brown, EdD, earned his BS and MEd from Frostburg State University, and his EdD in 2007 from West Virginia University. He holds certifications in administration, social studies, special education, and as a K–12 reading specialist in Maryland. He is currently the assistant supervisor of professional learning in Allegany County, Maryland, and he has taught several graduate-level courses as an adjunct instructor at West Virginia University since 2007. Dr. Brown has provided UDL trainings for employees of the Allegany County Public Schools and the Garrett County Public Schools. He also integrates the UDL principles and Guidelines in the graduate courses he teaches at West Virginia University. He has served as a guest lecturer on the topic at Frostburg State University, and he is the co-creator of an MSDE-certified two-credit course titled "The No Tech, Low Tech, and High Tech UDL Classroom."

William S. Burke, MS, currently serves as the Chief of Organizational Effectiveness for Baltimore County Public Schools (BCPS). Mr. Burke has worked for BCPS for twenty-three years as an elementary teacher, assistant principal, principal, executive director of professional development, and assistant superintendent. He holds a master of science degree from The Johns Hopkins University in Education and Administration. In his current role at BCPS, Mr. Burke oversees the Office of Organizational Development and the Office of Equity and Cultural Proficiency. He is currently providing strategic planning and support for the following district initiatives: UDL, redesigning teacher preparation, teacher and principal evaluation, peer assistance and review, cultural competency and an equity policy, the development of an applied health sciences magnet for grades 6–12, and a 1-to-1 device rollout and digital learning platform for all students in BCPS.

Lisa Carey, MAT, graduated from St. Mary's College of Maryland with a BA in history and received her master of arts in teaching from Goucher College, with dual certification in special education and social studies education. In 2013, she completed her Administrator One Certification through Towson University. Before she was accepted as one of the inaugural fellows at the Center for Innovation and Leadership in Special Education, Ms. Carey was a special education teacher in St. Mary's and Baltimore counties, where she specialized in inclusion practices for students with emotional-behavioral and developmental disabilities. She has taught as an adjunct special education faculty member at St. Mary's College of Maryland and Towson University. Ms. Carey joined the Center for Innovation as an education consultant in 2014, where she provides consultation and training services to educators, researchers, and clinicians to promote best practices in the field of special education.

Denise DeCoste, EdD, is an occupational therapist and a special educator with extensive experience in the field of assistive technology (AT). For two decades, Dr. DeCoste led AT teams for the Montgomery County Public Schools (MCPS) in Maryland. She provides professional learning on AT for reading and writing, on the restructuring of AT team services to build capacity, and to school districts across the United States. She has authored publications on augmentative communication, on AT to support reading and writing, and on AT services in school settings. Dr. DeCoste is also strongly invested in UDL. She was instrumental in building awareness of UDL and in the early phases of its implementation in MCPS schools. In 2010, she was the governor-appointed chair of the Maryland UDL Task Force, which led to the approval to incorporate UDL principles into the Code of Maryland Regulations. Dr. DeCoste currently is the vice chair of the UDL-Implementation Research Network; she has chaired two successful UDL-IRN summits and is actively involved in UDL-IRN operations.

Nicole Fiorito, MEd, currently works for Baltimore County Public Schools, where she holds the position of S.T.A.T. teacher at Halstead Academy of Art and Science in Parkville, Maryland. As the S.T.A.T. teacher, Ms. Fiorito provides professional development and coaching to teachers. She previously held positions as a classroom teacher at various grade levels and as a consulting teacher. She received a bachelor's degree from St. Mary's College of Maryland and a master's degree from Towson University.

Nancy S. Grasmick, PhD, is co-director of the Kennedy Krieger Institute, an internationally recognized institution dedicated to improving the lives of children and young adults with pediatric developmental disabilities and disorders of the brain, spinal cord, and musculoskeletal system, through patient care, special education, research, and professional training. Dr. Grasmick is also a presidential scholar at Towson University. Dr. Grasmick served as Maryland's first female state superintendent of schools. Under her leadership, the state of Maryland received one of the federal government's coveted Race to the Top education grants (2010), worth up to $250 million to continue building upon a solid record of school reform. During that time, Maryland received a number one ranking in the 2009, 2010, and 2011 Quality Counts report as the country's most consistently high-performing state. Also, for a third year in a row, Maryland's advanced placement performance was ranked #1 nationwide. The recipient of numerous awards, Dr. Grasmick began her career as a teacher of deaf children at the William S. Baer School in Baltimore City. She subsequently served as a teacher, principal, supervisor, assistant superintendent, and associate superintendent in Baltimore County Public Schools. Dr. Grasmick holds a doctorate from The Johns Hopkins University, a master's degree from Gallaudet University, and a bachelor's degree from Towson University.

Tina Greene, MEd, has been employed by the Bartholomew Consolidated School Corporation for nineteen years as UDL coordinator, with an emphasis on positive behavior instructional supports (PBIS) and instructional consultation and teaming (ICT). Ms. Greene's roles and responsibilities have included classroom instruction in kindergarten and first grade, ICT facilitation and case management, ICT district coordinator, and PBIS coach. She collaborates with her peers on the implementation of UDL, PBIS, and ICT within the district. Ms. Greene earned her bachelor's degree in elementary education from Indiana State University and her master's degree from Indiana Wesleyan University.

Marsye Kaplan, MS, CCC-SLP, ATP, is a speech language pathologist with more than forty years of experience working with children with disabilities. She is the Specialized Instruction Section Chief at the Maryland State Department of Education. Ms. Kaplan spent twenty-two years building the assistive technology program in a large school district while leading the UDL initiative for all students. She was granted the Maryland Outstanding Technology Leader in Education Award in 2012. She makes presentations on various assistive technology and UDL initiatives locally and nationally. Ms. Kaplan is also an adjunct instructor at Johns Hopkins and Towson universities.

Lisa Katz, MLS, is a professional educator, instructional designer, and facilitator specializing in design thinking, online course development, and mobile applications to support innovative teaching and learning. Ms. Katz applies design thinking, instructional design skills, and creativity to program management and learning design. She holds a BA in history education from the University of Delaware and an MLS from the University of Maryland, College Park. Ms. Katz began her education career as a secondary social studies teacher, became an instructional specialist at the MSDE, and led the teacher education program at the University of Maryland College Park. She is currently a digital learning specialist for Howard County Public Schools, where she works with teachers, administrators, and curriculum specialists to redesign curriculum for digital delivery, applying UDL instructional design principles to professional learning opportunities and the curating of digital content. Ms. Katz has led several mobile and digital learning projects for K–12, and created and implemented innovative practices for both the education market and the private sector. She has worked with both private industry and school districts in seven states to facilitate professional learning design for leadership teams, district administration, curriculum specialists, and school-based staff. Ms. Katz is passionate about innovation in education, and she believes that every conversation is an opportunity to engage and innovate to enrich learning experiences.

Rhonda J. Laswell, MEd, is the coordinator of Universal Design for Learning for Bartholomew Consolidated School Corporation. Before serving as the UDL coordinator, Ms. Laswell was a middle school science teacher. In her role as coordinator, she is responsible for the design and facilitation of staff professional development, consultations for curriculum and learning environment design, and the integration of PBIS. Ms. Laswell has attended the Harvard UDL Summer Institute and participated in UDL facilitators training at CAST, in conjunction with the UDL Professional Development System Project funded by the Bill & Melinda Gates Foundation.

Jennifer Mullenax, MEd, earned her bachelor's degree in elementary education from Towson University and her master's degree in leadership and supervision from Goucher College. She is currently pursuing her doctorate in education at Towson. After serving in various positions, including classroom teacher and central office administrator, Ms. Mullenax was appointed principal of Halstead Academy in 2010. At that time, Halstead was considered a failing school and was one year away from restructuring. In the five years Ms. Mullenax has served as Halstead's principal, she has revitalized the educational programs through her vision of what is possible and her ability to bring stakeholders together to work toward that vision. Halstead Academy, a Title One school, has closed the achievement gap and improved test scores, and parent involvement is at an all-time high. Halstead Academy now serves as a Lighthouse School, which means that teachers from 107 elementary school across the county can come to Halstead to observe model student-centered instruction. Halstead is also a professional development learning center that has partnered with Towson University to help re-create the university's teacher prep program. Ms. Mullenax has been recognized as Magnet Principal of the Year for Region 2 and was most recently named BCPS Principal of the Year.

Nicole Norris, MEd, is the principal of the Lansdowne Middle School in Baltimore, Maryland. Mrs. Norris earned her bachelor's degree in elementary and special education at the University of Delaware and her master's degree in education in an at-risk student concentration at Goucher College. Before becoming an administrator, Mrs. Norris was a special educator in self-contained and inclusion classes in elementary and middle schools. She served as the principal of Lansdowne Middle School during both the Bill & Melinda Gates Foundation UDL implementation project and the Towson University Presidential Scholar UDL project. Mrs. Norris has presented nationally on the UDL implementation process, most recently at the Harvard Graduate School of Education UDL Summer Institute.

Kirsten Omelan, PhD, has worked in the field of special education for more than fifteen years. She is currently an education specialist in the Special Education Department at the Region 4 Education Service Center in Texas, where she is the lead for Access to the General Curriculum initiatives. Ms. Omelan has practical experience as a special education teacher, department chair, and supervisor for special education programming in K–12 settings. She conducts professional development, provides coaching, creates resources, and supports multiyear UDL implementation efforts for several campuses and districts throughout the region.

Patricia Kelly Ralabate, EdD, is the author of *Your UDL Lesson Planner: The Step-by-Step Guide to Teaching All Learners* (Brookes Publishing, 2016). After completing a Boston College UDL postdoctoral fellowship, she served as director of implementation CAST, director of the National Center on UDL, a National UDL Task Force co-chair, and director of the Bill & Melinda Gates Foundation–funded project that focused on implementing UDL district-wide and on professional learning plans for four school systems. Building on twenty-five years of teaching experience as a speech-language pathologist and nine years as the National Education Association senior policy analyst for special and gifted education, Dr. Ralabate is a part-time faculty member at the George Washington University and facilitates CAST's online courses in UDL for English language learners.

Kavita Rao, PhD, is an associate professor in the College of Education at the University of Hawai'i at Mānoa. Dr. Rao teaches undergraduate and graduate courses on assistive and instructional technologies, and UDL to preservice and in-service teachers. She also conducts professional development on UDL for school districts in the United States and internationally. Dr. Rao's research focuses on assistive and instructional technologies, UDL, designing accessible online learning environments, and technology-related strategies for English language learners and other culturally and linguistically diverse students. Dr. Rao's prior professional experience includes working as a school technology coordinator in Massachusetts and as an educational technology specialist for Pacific Resources for Education and Learning in Honolulu. She has worked conducting professional development on technology and inclusive curriculum design with state education agencies and schools in Hawaii, Guam, American Samoa, the Commonwealth of the Northern Marianas Islands, Palau, Republic of the Marshall Islands, and the Federated States of Micronesia. Dr. Rao received her bachelor's degree from the University of North Carolina at Chapel Hill and her master's degree and PhD from the University of Hawai'i.

William A. Sadera, PhD, is a professor of instructional technology at Towson University. Dr. Sadera is a graduate of Iowa State University and has been a faculty member at Towson since 2000. Dr. Sadera is the director of the Instructional Technology Doctoral Program and conducts research in pre-service and in-service teacher technology preparation, the role of conceptual change and professional development, effective technology integration for learning, UDL, and distance education.

Rene Sanchez, MEd, is from Edinburg, which is located in the Rio Grande Valley of Texas. Upon graduating from high school, Mr. Sanchez earned his BA at the University of Notre Dame, his law degree at The Ohio State University, and his MEd in educational administration at the University of Texas. Rene has served in charter, private, and public schools, both rural and urban, where he has held diverse positions: teacher, coach, director, assistant principal, college counselor, admissions officer, grant coordinator, STEM director, accountability officer, and principal. He is currently the principal of César E. Chávez High School in the Houston Independent School District. Mr. Sanchez believes that all students can learn, a belief driven by the contexts of place and story, which together allow students to weave tales through text, speech, drawing, music, or code and enable them to make connections for their own learning. He also believes that the entire school system—from the school board, to the superintendent, to the principals, to the teachers—must tap into those connections to engage students.

Christina J. Schindler, MS, has spent the last fourteen years in both college and K–12 settings, where she effectively integrated technology into the classroom to support all learners. Mrs. Schindler is currently employed by the Queen Anne's County Public Schools as a facilitator of digital teaching and learning. In this role, she provides universally designed instructional support and technology training to support all students, teachers, and staff. Mrs. Schindler has an administration certification and is a certified special education, general education, and history education teacher, as well as a Google-certified teacher. She earned an MS in educational technology from The College of New Jersey. In 2015, Mrs. Schindler was selected to serve as a Universal Design for Learning Leadership Fellow through the Office of the Presidential Scholar at Towson University.

Susan Spinnato, MEd, has been a teacher and curriculum/professional development specialist for more than forty years, and is currently the director of instructional programs at the MSDE. Before joining MSDE, she was the coordinator of world languages and ESOL for BCPS.

George Van Horn, EdD, is the director of special education for the Bartholomew Special Services Cooperative in Columbus, Indiana, and a member of the CAST UDL faculty cadre. Dr. Van Horn completed both his bachelor of science and master of science degrees at the University of Dayton. He received his doctor of education degree from Indiana University, with a concentration in school administration and special education. Dr. Van Horn has been a teacher of students with emotional disabilities and has served as a principal, school superintendent, and director of special education. Dr. Van Horn has also been an adjunct faculty member at Indiana University, Purdue University Columbus, Manhattan College in New York, and Northern Illinois University. He has consulted with school districts throughout the country in the areas of PBIS, UDL, and inclusion.

Jessica Vogel, MAT, just completed her eighth year as the assistant director of special education for Bartholomew Consolidated School Corporation. She previously was a special education teacher and coordinator at both the elementary and middle school levels. While teaching, she worked collaboratively with general education teachers to co-teach and implement the principles of UDL. Ms. Vogel has been a Council for Exceptional Children (CEC) member for more than fourteen years, and she has served as the secretary and president of the Indiana CEC. She completed her bachelor of science in education degree from Indiana University–Bloomington and her master of arts in teaching degree from Oakland City University, with a concentration in building administration. Ms. Vogel also earned her special education director license at Indiana University–Bloomington.

Angie Wieneke, MLS, has been employed with the Bartholomew Consolidated School Corporation for seventeen years, currently as Universal Design for Learning Coordinator, with emphasis on instructional media technology. Ms. Wieneke's roles and responsibilities have included first-grade teacher, high school media specialist, supervisor of the elementary library programs, and instructional technology. Through her work with UDL and instructional media technology, Ms. Wieneke provides many opportunities for professional development, helps the elementary library assistants provide a UDL-rich learning environment in the elementary libraries, and is involved with many technology committees in the Bartholomew Consolidated School Corporation.

Acknowledgments

I am most grateful to the staff at CAST, especially the wise and patient David Gordon, for supporting this work from its inception. Numerous CAST staff members were highly engaged in many of the projects described in this book, and I am thankful for the opportunity to share our implementation work with a wider audience. The chapter authors in this book represent some of the most talented, innovative, and dedicated leaders that I have had the pleasure to work with and learn from. I appreciate the time you all have dedicated to this book, even when it may have distracted you from your primary roles. David Rose, Grace Meo, and Tom Hehir have challenged many of the authors to "change the world" by looking through a UDL lens and creating an equitable learning environment for all children. It is an honor for us to carry on your work.

Being the mother of two of the greatest girls in the world and engaging in the important implementation work described in this book would not be possible without the support and encouragement of my husband Ben and my parents, Jeff and Debi Tessier, and my grandmother, Nancy Lang. Thank you for your commitment to our girls and to all of the learners who will benefit from the implementation of UDL. I have had the privilege to learn and grow alongside many amazing teachers and leaders as we have refined our understanding of UDL and helped schools and districts realize that we are more effective when we work together. Many of you contributed to this book, but all of you contributed to the important work of moving UDL from awareness to implementation: Kirk Behnke, Courtney Bensch, Billy Burke, Lisa Carey,

Peggy Coyne, Denise DeCoste, Nancy Grasmick, Kay Holman, Bill Jensen, Marsye Kaplan, Lisa Katz, Kirsten Omelan, Grace Meo, Jessica Moore, Loui Lord Nelson, Betsy Neville, Nikki Norris, Katie Novak, Jaime Oakley, Patti Ralabate, Sandra Reid, David Rose, Rene Sanchez, George Van Horn—you are all the BEST. When all leaders model your work ethic, passion, and dedication to all kids, their learning will truly have no limits.

—ELIZABETH BERQUIST, Editor

Index